Historic Cheeses

LEICESTERSHIRE, STILTON & STICHELTON

Webster's dairy at Saxelbye, where Stilton cheese is produced. The dairy is part of the House of Callow, a cheese dairy and Deli wholesaler. Callow park dairy were producing Leicester cheese off Church Street and Wharf Street, Leicester, in the 1920s. In the foreground Leicester and Stilton cheese are featured with an early 20th-century Stilton hoop and a Leicester cheese mould.

Historic Cheeses
LEICESTERSHIRE, STILTON & STICHELTON

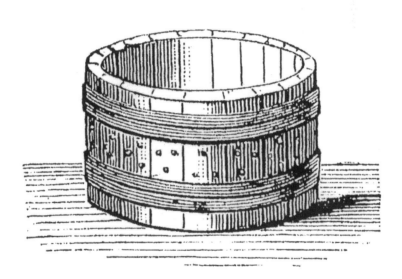

TREVOR HICKMAN

The Corn Exchange, c.1920. The original Exchange was built in 1748. The main use of this building was to store cheese, especially large 'wheels' of Leicestershire cheese. In 1850 the building was demolished to cater for the expanding corn market, which was offered for the daily sale of Lincolnshire corn. Bartering and the sale of produce from the Market Place dates back over 1,000 years. This photograph was taken just after World War One, and shows the sale of locally produced goods and, of course, 'fruits from the Empire'.

An engraving of a tympanum in a Norman arch at the church of Stoney Stanton, as it appeared in 1788. It depicts a shepherd with his sheep, a dog defending his master from the devil (symbolised by a dragon) and an eagle overlooking the scene.

First published in Great Britain in 2009 by
The Breedon Books Publishing Company Limited
Breedon House, 3 The Parker Centre,
Derby, DE21 4SZ. ISBN 978-1-85983-736-8

Paperback edition published in Great Britain in 2012 by
The Derby Books Publishing Company Limited
3 The Parker Centre, Derby, DE21 4SZ.

Half-title page: Bewick's engraving of mediaeval sheep.

Title page engraving: A wooden Stilton cheese mould.

ISBN 978-1-78091-111-3
Printed and bound by CPI Group (UK) Ltd, Croydon, CR0 4YY

Contents

9   Chapter One: Cheese in Leicestershire

25   Chapter Two: Leicestershire Cheese

45   Chapter Three: The Cheese Wars

55   Chapter Four: Red Leicester

75   Chapter Five: Stilton Cheese

135   Chapter Six: Stichelton

157   Postscript

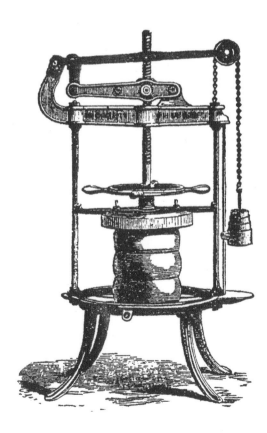

A depiction of a cheese press, dating from c.1870, which shows three Leicestershire cheeses under pressure.

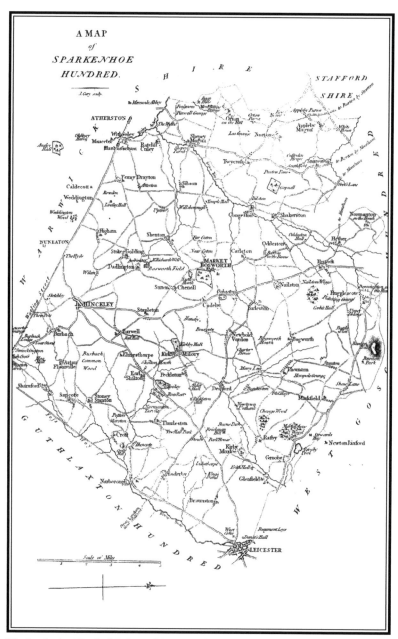

The Sparkenhoe Hundred, Leicestershire, was a cheese producing district. This engraving of the area by John Cary was produced in 1810. Sparkenhoe Hundred was formed by King Edward III between 1327 and 1377 by reducing part of the Gathlaxton Hundred. It is interesting to note that Ansley Hall in Warwickshire is featured.

Chapter One

Cheese in Leicestershire

*I*n 1994 I was invited to write a history of the development of Stilton cheese and now, because of increased interest in the history of the cheese being produced in Leicestershire and Nottinghamshire, I have compiled this book.

Evidence suggests that cheese has been made in England for well over 4,000 years. The first cheese-makers would have been the farmers of the Neolithic period (between *c.*4000 and 2400 BC), and the first cheese was, in truth, probably made by accident. According to the few pieces of evidence that have survived, cheese was first produced in the Middle East, possibly in the area now comprising Turkey and Iran. Did some wandering traveller place his daily supply of milk in a bag made of animal skin with some offal still inside it, mount his beast of burden and travel along the highway, with the animal's movement and the hot sun separating the curd from the whey and the liquid draining out through a hole in the bag? Was this how the first crude cheese was produced? We can but speculate. However, we do know that by the time of the Romans cheese was part of the staple diet of the marching Roman legions, the Mediterranean invaders that conquered and occupied England for almost 400 years, as it is repeatedly referred to in Roman cookery books. Archaeological surveys have indicated that Leicestershire was farmed by numerous Romano-British communities. They would have raised cows, goats and sheep, and they would have made cheese.

Julius Caesar attacked England in 55 BC. In AD 43 the Emperor Claudius invaded Britain in an attempt to occupy the whole of the country; his victorious fleet sailed up the River Thames and founded Londinium, and to consolidate their conquests the Roman occupiers built a system of roadways. One such road was Ermine Street, constructed to stretch from Londinium to Hadrian's Wall, with the Fosse Way (from Bath) and Watling Street connecting the West Midlands to London. The major routes intersected at a crossroads at High Cross, a few miles to the south-west of the town of Hinckley. The roads were designed to carry horse-drawn carts, chariots, cavalry and soldiers on foot.

An overnight camp was laid out approximately 70 miles north of London at Stilton on Ermine Street and a major Roman camp was constructed at High Cross. At the site of the camp, located near the present village of Stilton, in the spring of 2006, Richard Landy, a local professional potter, found a complete Roman cheese mould. The Romans produced many types of cheese made from ewes' milk obtained from the native sheep. A rennet was made by boiling nettles in water and adding the liquid to the milk in a wooden trough. When the milk had curdled, the curd was cut into small pieces, the whey strained off and the curd pressed into the mould. Holes in the base allowed excess whey to drain off. After two days the solid cream cheese was removed from the mould and placed on racks on a bed of nettles, then wrapped in nettle leaves. It would have been ready for eating after two weeks. The ordinary stinging nettle, *Urtica dioica*, was important to the Romans, who considered this plant very beneficial for digestion.

On a site on Watling Street, near Atherstone, a large Roman trading site was erected across the highway and given the name Manduessedum (Mancetter). From this Roman town a road was constructed to Ratae (Leicester). From the evidence that has survived, it can be said that Leicester became a leading city in the area during the Roman occupation. The remains of cheese-making moulds have been found during the many archaeological excavations centred on Mancetter and also at a Roman fort at Bainbridge in Yorkshire. The Roman scribe Pliny the Younger referred to imported cheese:

'. . .of cheese brought here from across the seas [...]

is justly famous. There is salt in pastures that produce cheese. . .'

The cheese produced by the Romans would today be classed as 'slipcoat' cheese. A slipcoat cheese was the earliest form of cheese, a very simple cheese that did not have a very long 'shelf life' and quickly turned blue-veined. The story of the origins of Roquefort could have a parallel in the production of the first blue-veined cheese. Legend has it that a group of French peasants were grazing their flocks high up in the Cevennes mountains (where this famous French cheese is still made) when they were surprised by some brigands who drove off their

An engraving showing a reproduction of the Roman Emperor Claudius from one of his circulated coins. c.AD 45.

flocks. The shepherds fled, returning days later to look for their abandoned *fromagen*, a soft cheese made from ewes' milk and bread. Their frugal meal was still hidden where they had left it and had developed a firm crust with blue mould running through the mixture. Their hunger pangs were so great that they made a meal out of what had survived, and to their surprise they found it very palatable. This was the type of cheese that the Romans ate and enjoyed, and unquestionably cream cheese was produced throughout the East Midlands and exported to Rome. They also pressed their cream cheese to remove the excess whey so that it travelled longer distances without breaking down.

The word 'cheese' is derived from the Latin word *caseus*. In England, before AD 1100 it was called *cyse*, this later became *cease*, and in the 16th and 17th centuries it became known as *ches* or *chiese*. The earliest written reference book mentioning cheese in England was compiled by the master of cooks to Richard II in 1390 as part of a manuscript volume of recipes entitled *The Forme of Cury, a Roll of Ancient English Cookery*. It was first published as a printed book in 1781 and contains a recipe in which grated cheese is added to soup.

To produce good-quality milk the correct type of soil is essential, and the best cheese has always been made from the milk of cows that graze on good pasture. Without good grass it is impossible to obtain the quality, and above all the quantity, that is so necessary to produce fine cheese. The first domesticated cattle were of a different breed to those encountered today, being semi-wild with small udders. The Romans bred new strains, but after they left Britain their influence on agriculture deteriorated. There was a considerable climate change as the British Isles entered a period of extreme cold that lasted for many centuries. The easiest farm animal to raise was the hardy local sheep, with its thick woollen coat coming in handy for making warm clothing. The native farmers used these animals to produce milk in the spring and early summer months.

Changes took place when the Anglo-Saxons integrated with the Romano-British and introduced different methods of agriculture, and further changes occurred after the Danes conquered and occupied parts of England. Sheep were still the main source of farming income. The Saxons increased their flocks of sheep as ewes' milk and wool were essential commodities. The Saxons and Danes farmed the fields of the East Midlands for nearly 700 years and certainly

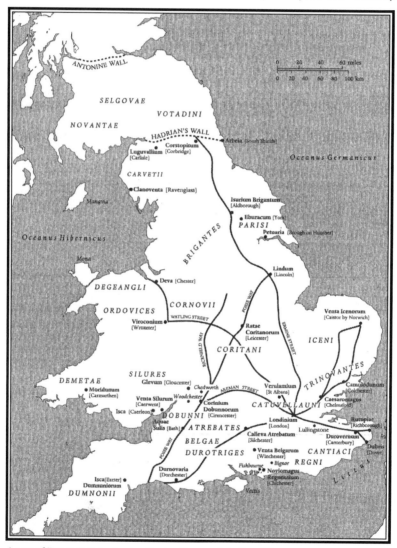

A map of Roman Britain showing Ermine Street and the Fosse Way.

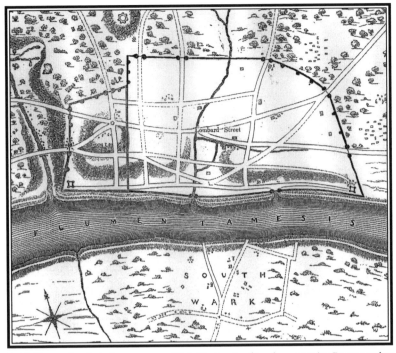

In 1860 an archaeological survey was published in the city of London concerning Roman markets held in Londinium. From a 21st-century standpoint the accuracy of this survey is questionable. However, the Victorians were of the opinion that markets were organised off the River Fleet, which was connected with Lombard Street, Cornhill. They believed goods were conveyed down the tributaries of the River Fleet to the River Thames and on to Rome. The survey's results can be seen in this 19th-century plan.

considered cheese to be an important part of their diet. The Scandinavian invaders introduced a breed of cattle into England that eventually gave rise to the strain known as Lincoln Reds. These cattle are noted for their size and hardiness, and they are dual-purpose, being raised for beef production and seasonal milk yields. It was this breed that became the common cow of the Nottinghamshire, Leicestershire and Lincolnshire wolds.

The next major development in agriculture came with the Norman Conquest in 1066, following which William the Conqueror divided up England, granting vast areas of his new kingdom to his victorious generals. It is interesting to note that in the *Domesday Book* of 1086, compiled on the instructions of William I, the village of Stilton was divided into three districts in the Hundred of Norman Cross: one was under the control of the king, one under the control of Eustace,

An engraving published in 1860 of the tessellated pavement uncovered in Lombard Street c.1780.
It was considered to be the home of a Roman merchant trading out of Londinium.

the king's sheriff of the county of 'Huntedunscire', while the other was controlled by the Bishop of Lincoln. The landowners endowed large tracts of farmland to provide support for various abbeys, monasteries, priories and churches throughout England.

Cheese was an essential food throughout the mediaeval period. All the religious houses received tithe and taxes, which were paid into their system of administration to support their work with the poor and assist in maintaining Christianity in an agricultural district. Cheese made from surplus milk by any villager who could support a cow, and from the cows and large flocks of sheep owned by the lord of the manor, would have been an easy commodity to transport as tithe because it would not deteriorate to the same extent as other edible products. Indeed, as it aged it often improved in quality! Friars and monks attached to the religious houses more often than not also served as farm labourers; they reared cows for milk and would certainly have had a surplus, which would then be made into cheese. Because hospitality was a feature of most monastic orders, cheese would be offered as standard fare for all travellers and incumbents residing in religious establishments in this area of the Midlands. It is hardly likely that any form of milk collection existed, and all milk would have been produced on site.

The animals which produced the milk in sufficient quantity for cheese to be made during the mediaeval period were ewes. Vast flocks of sheep roamed the rolling plains of the shire counties and some were contained in hurdles on common land. Cheese was a seasonal product, controlled by natural forces such as drought and famine years. The terrible famine that devastated the Midlands in 1316 would have decimated the sheep and cattle populations of the shires, and it would have taken decades to recover from the disaster. Very little cheese of any kind would have been available as there was no surplus milk. It is fairly certain that the cheese produced in the mediaeval period was small in size and weight (not unlike rounded 'baby Stiltons' that are marketed today) and made from ewes' or cows' milk. These early cheeses were unpressed. Instead the curd was wrapped in linen cloths, the whey was squeezed out and then the pouches were hung up to drain. To speed up the process, weights were placed on the cloth bags that were stacked on shelves, thus ensuring that the whey drained away more quickly. This method was eventually superseded by a purpose-built press. Unpressed cheese was made side-by-side with pressed cheese, and unpressed cheese developed blue mould very quickly between the crumbled curds. The curd was eventually packed into a hoop and stacked on a hastener.

Established religious houses at this time supported only one or two milking cows. It was not until the reign of Henry VII, commencing in 1485, that considerable change took place. This king encouraged trade, not war, and rural agricultural districts became more stable. The monastic orders became involved in village administration to an enormous extent, gaining wealth and power in the process. Their involvement in producing and marketing food so increased that it was one of the contributing factors to their eventual downfall.

Under the feudal system, lords of the manor and their farmers – peasants – organised the tilling of the soil, rotation of crops and the raising of animals for slaughter and milk production. Tithes were paid to the overlord and to the religious houses in turn.

In 1509 an 18-year-old King Henry VIII ascended the throne after the death of his father. He ruled a turbulent England that was always short of money, and he brought about the Dissolution of the Monasteries in 1536. This act changed the course of agriculture throughout England. When he acquired the religious lands owned by the church, he sold off his acquisitions to private individuals who could afford the price. Those landowners who were still in favour with the king retained their holdings and became even wealthier.

One family of landowners who benefitted from these measures were the Berkeleys. On the conquest of England in 1066 William I had granted large areas of land to his generals. Leicester and the majority of west Leicestershire were granted to Hugh de Grantmesnil. Parts of East Leicestershire and Rutland were granted to Henry de Ferrers, who built a castle in Tutbury, and de Grantmesnil built a castle in Leicester. The de Ferrers were good politicians and they expanded their holdings, granting large tracts of land to the county knights, mainly through marriage. The Hamelins were related to the de Ferrers and through marriage to the Berkeleys, whose castle was in Gloucestershire. Today the Berkeleys still reside in this castle. The de Grantmesnils did not co-operate with the reigning king and were at war with William II (Rufus), and over the following centuries the de Grantmesnil farmland was re-distributed to various individuals. However, as late as 1785 it is marked on a map indicating 'the old Park of Hugh Grantmesnil', south of the town of Hinckley, prior to the enclosure awards.

Henry de Ferrers, the first Duke of Derby. This woodcut was produced in the 17th century. William I granted de Ferrers vast areas of land throughout the Midlands. He built a castle at Tutbury in about 1068. Part of the holding was the village of Wymondham in Leicestershire. Eventually, through marriage, this came into the possession of the Hamelins, and then again through marriage to the Berkeley family. They enclosed the open fields in the early 16th century.

The enclosure awards changed the method of agriculture throughout the whole of the shire counties. Mediaeval monastic enclosures commenced the process, followed by the lords of the manor, then central government completed the procedure with the Enclosure Acts of the 1760s.

In east Leicestershire soft cream cheese maintained precedence over pressed cheese, mainly because of large-scale land ownership, particularly by the Berkeleys, who enclosed large tracts of land in and around the parish of Wymondham. The Berkeleys were keen farmers and added to their land holdings, establishing farming controls. In the 1560s they set about enclosing the common land in the parish of Wymondham by building walls and ditching and hedging it for their own use, evicting the local farmers. In terms of the rearing of cattle, these measures allowed the Berkeleys more control of their cows and selective breeding. Better feeding methods, from fodder produced in managed meadows, led to higher yields of milk and thus cheese

Hugh de Grantmesnil. William I granted part of Leicestershire to this knight, who built a castle in Leicester in 1068. This sketch was produced in the early 20th century from a stained-glass window in the church of the Abbey of St Evroult, in northern France, where his body was interred in 1098.

production increased. By then Maurice Berkeley controlled more cattle than any of his forebears. A number of villagers petitioned King Henry VIII against the restrictive measures put in place by the family, but to no avail. The open-field system was still in operation in the parishes close to Melton Mowbray and throughout Leicestershire to the south, but this method of farming was not conducive to producing surplus milk. The situation did not change until the Enclosure Acts of the 1760s. J. Houghton, in his book *A Collection for the Importance*

In 1661 Charles II (1660–1685) gave instructions that all statutes which parliament considered the law of the land should be published. Seven Acts of Parliament were involved in the marketing of cheese. They had become law during the reigns of Henry VI, Edward VI, Philip and Mary and James I. Two of the published Acts of Parliament are printed below. There were many other acts of parliament that were not recorded in this statute.

Anno nono Henrici sexti.

ITem, whereas it hath béen of old times accustomed in all the Counties of England, that all the Chéses which ought to be sold by the Waiey should be weighed by the Auncel, and because that at the last parliament holden at Westminster, it was ordained, that the said Auncels in respect of the great deceit of the same should be destroyed, and other weights touching should be in this behalf ordained, and it is so, that the poor people of the realm be greatly deceibed by the said weights touching, for that they know not how many pounds the Waiey of Chéese doth contain, by the said weights touching. And therefore to the intent that the said poor people shall not be in this behalf deceibed, as they habe béen sithence the said last Parliament: It is ordained by authority of this Parliament, that the weight of a Waiey of Chéese may contain xxxij. clobes, that is to say, ebery clobe vij. li. by the said weights touching.

Henry VI in 1430 (1422–1461).

Anno quinto & sexto Edwardi sexti.

BE it enacted by the authority of this present Parliament, that no person or persons after the feast of the Annunciation of our Lady next coming, shall buy to sell again any Butter or Chéese, unlesse he or they sell the same again by retail in open Shop, fair or Market, and not in grosse, upon pain of forfeiture of the double value of the same Butter and Chéese so sold, contrary to the tenor of this present Act: the one moity of all which forfeiture to be to our Soberaign Lord the King, his heirs and successors, and the other moity to him or them that will sue for the same in any of the Kings courts of Record, wherein no wager of law, essoin or protection shall be allowed for the defendant or defendants.

Provided alwayes, and be it enacted by the authority aforesaid, that the said word of retail mentioned in this Act, shall be expounded, declared and taken, onely where a weight of Chéese, or a barrel of Butter, or of lesse quantity, and not abobe, shall be sold at any time to any person or persons in open Shop, fair or Market, and that to be done without fraud or cobin.

Provided alway, that this Act, or any thing therein contained, shall not extend to any Inholder or Victualer, for such Butter or Chéese as shall be spent or uttered by retail, in any of their houses, any thing contained in this Act to the contrary notwithstanding: this Act to endure to the next Parliament.

Edward VI in 1549 (1547–1553).

of Husbandry and Trade, published in 1727, states: 'Among them [cows] a great many small ones, which are hardly worth the keeping, but the encouragement is, and many pernicious commons we have which, for the flush of milk in a few summer months, makes the poor buy cows, to starve them in winter and to spend so much time running after them as would earn twice the worth of their milk by an ordinary manufacture; when as, if the commons were enclosed, some would feed them well all summer […] whereby there would always be a tolerable plenty of milk, from which would spring many more considerable dairies.'

It was not until Charles Colling and Robert Bakewell began breeding experiments in the 18th century, assisted by alterations to the methods of feeding cattle introduced by Lord ('Turnip') Townsend (1674–1738), that improved milk yields from cows allowed the mass production of cheese. Until the early 18th century it was very much a seasonal commodity made from spare milk. Cheese production was then expanded throughout the country in the early 18th century.

Without a good rennet the manufacture of cheese is impossible. Rennet is the essential agent needed to coagulate milk to produce curd. Rennin is the active enzyme involved, and it is found in the stomach walls of mammals, with the greatest concentration being in the rumen of an unweaned calf.

Throughout Leicestershire vegetable rennet was the main source of coagulation, and the wives of the farmers who traded in cheese often maintained a herb garden growing little else but 'Lady's Bedstraw'. Many cheese-makers grew this as a herb, solely for the production of cheese. Gerarde, in his famous 1597 herbal, stated that the peasants called it 'cheese-renning' and that the finest Cheshire cheese was produced using Lady's Bedstraw. From this plant, *Galcum verum*, a yellow dye can be produced, and the roots produce a bright red dye. Combined, the flowers and the root produce an excellent rennet, coagulating the milk to produce a deep orange/red cheese – the Leicestershire cheese. The red dye from the root was used for a variety of purposes, especially dyeing cloth. In the Leicestershire Museum's survey of flora in the county in 1988, it is recorded that Lady's Bedstraw was 'Frequent throughout the county in old grassland'.

There was some opposition to the use of annatto, which comes from the soft pulpy seeds of a small tree that grows in South America called *Bixa orellana*, as a colouring agent; carotene from carrots was preferred, especially as it contained vitamin A, while annatto has little

Woodcut from Schweizer Chronik *by J. Stumf, 1548. This is possibly the earliest printed illustration showing the practice of cheese-making.*

King Edward III (1327–1377). This king supported the formation of local markets for the sale and bartering of goods produced in the open fields.

or no benefit other than its deep colour. Animal rennet was a European rennet occasionally used in England, and it became more popular towards the end of the 18th century.

In the 1920s and 1930s salted calves' stomachs were imported into England from Poland, packed in small barrels. These 'vels' were then washed to remove excess salt, turned inside out and soaked for a few days. The resulting liquid, the rennet, was then stored in earthenware jars. This form of supply was acceptable to the large manufacturers of cheese, while many small farm dairies still purchased calves' paunches direct from the local slaughterhouse for immediate use.

Cheese was also produced using other methods besides calves' rennet and Lady's Bedstraw. Other vegetable products were also mixed with milk, so forming coagulation. In Leicestershire, nettles were boiled in water with salt, producing a rennet. Also used were goose grass and marsh marigold flowers. These were boiled in alum, along with nettle roots, which produced a yellow dye, that coagulated the milk and coloured the cheese.

A wooden slipcoat mould held in the Carnegie Museum at Melton Mowbray. A cheese made in this mould, when it consolidated, was wrapped in cabbage leaves for two weeks.

Eventually cheese-makers in Leicestershire who were providing the pressed coloured cheese preferred to use readily available rennet, as the process of combining separately produced rennet and colouring agent was a problem. Lady's Bedstraw coloured vegetable rennet had fallen out of favour and animal rennet was preferred. Many farmers obtained their own calves' rumens and produced their own rennet by combining these with annatto in a powdered form. Rumen 'vels' were imported as dried skins, and it was possible to soak these skins in water with annatto and market them to the respective farmers. In 1880 Richard Adkinson, a dealer in assorted cheeses, was recorded as selling 'cheese colouring skins' produced from calves' stomachs from his shop in Leicester.

Taste and the colour of cheese have always been important to the consumer. There are many different coloured cheeses in Leicestershire, including creamy white, creamy white/blue veined, yellow, orange and orange-red. In the 21st century a creamy, white blue-veined cheese – Stilton – takes precedence, while Red Leicestershire is another popular cheese produced in the county.

Marsh Marigold. The flowers produce a rennet when boiled with alum, which coagulates milk to make a deep yellow-coloured cheese.

Lady's Bedstraw. The flowers and leaves of this plant produce rennet when boiled, which was used to coagulate milk. The roots of the plant produce a red dye when boiled, and this was used in the colouring of Leicestershire cheese.

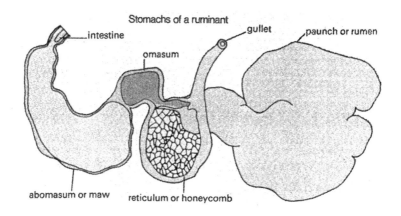

Rennet is needed to coagulate milk to produce curd. Rennin is the active enzyme found in the stomach walls of mammals, with the greatest concentration being in the rumen of an unweaned calf. It is used with annatto to produce Red Leicester cheese.

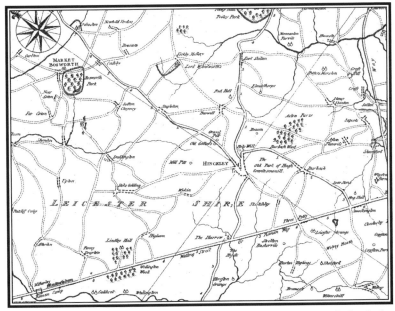

The open fields around Hinckley in 1785. This was a cheese-producing area in the Sparkenhoe Hundred. The enclosure awards were finally completed in this area in 1794.

A Roman cheese mould alongside a modern reproduction. This mould was found near the village of Stilton in 2006. With nettles acting as a rennet a soft cream cheese would have been produced, which would now be classed as slipcoat. The cheese would have been wrapped in nettles for two weeks until it was ready for consumption.

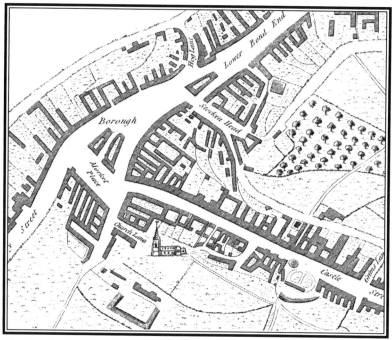

A map of the centre of Hinckley in 1782, with the large Market Place.

The base of a Leicestershire cheese press, which had been carved out of a slate headstone for a new purpose. It was re-erected in the churchyard of the Church of St John the Baptist at Old Dalby.

Chapter Two

Leicestershire Cheese

The ancient cheese of Leicestershire is unquestionably of a deep orange colour. The traditional cheese was a pressed Leicestershire cheese and was considered to be one of the finest produced in England in the early mediaeval period. There are many theories of how this cheese developed and was maintained in west Leicestershire.

Learned academics are of the opinion that when the Roman occupiers departed England after nearly 400 years their system of government collapsed, and in the main this is true for the urban structure of occupation. The slaves, peasants and the Romano-British, who were left in ownership of the vast farming structure that had developed, continued to cultivate the land and farms, and they continued to raise the cattle and sheep that were crucial for their survival. Neolithic, Bronze Age and Iron Age man, and the Romano-British, all produced cheese, and the practice continued after the departure of the Romans. In many areas of England pressed cheese continued to be produced, especially in west Leicestershire in and around Manduessedum, off Watling Street, and in the villages around Hinckley. It is amazing how many press blocks and circular carved base stones survive in the small isolated farms of the area. The original presses would have been quite small, and so the base stones that have survived are of 18th and 19th-century origin. The small pressed cheese would have been compacted by placing flat stones by hand on curd wrapped in linen, applying more stones to compress the cheese to remove the excess whey. Over the centuries stone heads controlled by a screw thread and stone base plates developed, similar to fruit and wine presses used on the Continent.

The Sparkenhoe Hundred, an area to the west of Leicester, was the main centre for cheese production. A number of wealthy landowners supported the manufacture of cheese, and the bartering and selling of their produce was crucial. This was undertaken in the large markets in Leicestershire. The most important and possibly the earliest market commenced at Manduessedum, and even when

William Shakespeare in 1623. His father dealt in farmhouse produce and possibly had dealings in Hinckley. William worked on his father's farm, with a particular interest in dairy products.

the Romans left some form of trade continued at the site. The Saxons traded in the area before the Norman Conquest, after which Hinckley developed as a leading market in the Midlands. Casual markets had been held for centuries, sometimes controlled by the religious houses in this district.

Traditionally cheeses were available in the Monday market in Hinckley and were usually purchased by the working class early on Monday morning, so that it was available as a daily food throughout the working week. The right to hold the Monday market in Hinckley was first granted by King Edward III to Blanche, the wife of the Duke of Lancaster, in perpetuity. The Duke had died during the Black Death on 13 July 1364. As lord of the manor he and his tenants were not required to pay 'lastage', a toll for the sale of produce at the markets in the county of Leicestershire. King Edward III had considerable sympathy for the underprivileged, especially the peasant class who farmed in the open fields of England. The villages and towns of Leicestershire had been decimated when the Black Death reached England in 1348 and one-third of the total population died over the next 12 months. Today the layout of deserted villages can be located throughout the county as grass-covered mounds.

The Dissolution of the Monasteries by Henry VIII changed all this as he took over all tolls and rents. When he died his young son held the crown for a very short time from the age of nine. The Duke of Somerset was appointed his protector and he influenced the young king. On 20 January 1551 he instructed the young Edward VI to award a grant so that a market could continue to be held on every Monday throughout the year. The first cheese fair with a royal grant was held in November 1551, although a cheese fair had taken place every November or late December from as far back as the 12th century, at which large quantities of pressed cheese had been available.

William Shakespeare (1564–1616) was well aware that the famous cheese fair existed at Hinckley, and it is, of course, possible that he visited Hinckley from his home in Warwickshire, a short horse ride away. William worked on his father's farm and records show that John Shakespeare ran a dairy, raising cows to produce milk.

On dairy farms such as the one John Shakespeare owned, only female calves were retained, while bull calves were killed to provide veal. One of William's duties was to kill the bull calves for his father, although we are told that he 'would do it in a high style and make a speech'! In the 1590s he published a number of his works. Interestingly, in the second part of one such work, Shakespeare's *Henry IV*, Justice Shallow is asked by his employee, Davy, if he means 'to stop any of William's wages about the sack he lost the other day at Hinckley fair.'

Cheese production took place throughout the county of Leicestershire; pressed cheese in the west, unpressed cream cheese in the east. Towards Melton Mowbray,

A Leicestershire Longhorn cow.

farmers and their wives produced pressed and unpressed cheese. Quenby Hall had an historic dairy, which first produced red-coloured pressed cheese. Today circular carved base stones have been laid out within the flagstone footpaths in the hall gardens, as a memento of pressed cheese production. In 1759 Stilton cheese was marketed from this dairy farm by Shuckburgh Ashby, who was one of the leading entrepreneurs of cheese production in Leicestershire.

The Shuckburgh family originates from Upper Shuckburgh, a small village in Warwickshire. Shuckburgh Hall, originally a half-timbered hall, was demolished and rebuilt in 1844. Richard Shuckburgh raised a troop of soldiers from his estate and supported Charles I at the battle of Edgehill, for which he was knighted, and he died in 1656. After his death the Shuckburghs took on double-barrelled names when they got married. In the church of St John the Baptist in this village there are a number of monuments to the Shuckburghs; for example, on the south side of the nave lies Lady Evelyn Shuckburgh.

In 1746 Shuckburgh Ashby purchased the lordship of Aston Flamville and all the recently enclosed fields from the Torville family, who had held the lordship

for many decades. This hamlet had obtained a national reputation for the quality of milk and cheese it produced from their local cows. Shuckburgh Ashby wished to expand his business in the profitable market of fine pressed cheese, and in 1752 he sold his farming estate in Aston Flamville to his grandson by marriage, Joseph Cradock. Shuckburgh Ashby then developed lands he held in Northamptonshire. In 1759 Quenby Hall came on the market and he purchased the estate from a member of his family. The previous owners of Quenby Hall had gained a reputation through leasing the estate as a dairy farm to John

A base of a cheese press in the 1890s, still in its original position at a farmhouse in the north Midlands.

Quenby Hall, c.1910. This was the home of Shuckburgh Ashby, who produced pressed Leicestershire cheese in a dairy at this hall in 1759. He then developed a fine Stilton cheese for sale at the 'Town of Stilton' on Ermine Street and Cornhill in London.

Oneby, who had leased part of this farm in 1664 and had marketed pressed cheese to London. After he purchased Quenby Hall, Shuckburgh Ashby expanded the production of the red-coloured pressed Leicestershire cheese and proceeded to develop his Stilton cheese under the guidance of Frances Pawlett from Wymondham. They soon expanded the scale of production and marketed the cheese for sale in Leicester, the small town of Stilton in Huntingdonshire and Cornhill in London, with help from the entrepreneur Cooper Thornhill.

Shuckburgh Ashby converted the ruinous large building standing near Quenby Hall into an extensive dairy, and he completed the enclosure of the surrounding open fields. He did this in order to be able to raise the Leicestershire longhorn cow developed by Robert Bakewell. In 1790 the average quantity of milk per cow was three gallons a day.

The Hinckley market was essential for the marketing of Sparkenhoe cheese. Queen Elizabeth I granted a Royal Charter in 1587 that on every Monday a market should be held in the centre of the town. She then decreed that after 28 October 1587 this would take place on the first Monday of the month. An annual cheese fair was also held on the site. It is interesting to note that very few cheese fairs were granted a Royal Charter. This is presumably why Shakespeare records the Hinckley fair and why the cheese market takes precedence over all markets concerning this produce in Leicestershire. Does it still apply? If so, it has precedence over the Stilton cheese market at Melton Mowbray that commenced in 1883. After this charter was granted, the running of the market passed into and through many hereditary families who were landowners, who were entitled to pay and receive assorted small rents, possibly connected to the site, on various produce stalls. The borough collected the rents payable to the king (or queen) via the Duchy of Lancaster. On 29 November 1764 Elizabeth and Shuckburgh Ashby made a donation to the town by removing the rights of entitlement to receive tolls for the sale of produce in the market that was due from their tenants in and around Hinckley. It is possible that Ashby purchased the right to do so from the Duchy.

Shuckburgh Ashby was a large landowner, and he and his family owned estates throughout Leicestershire, Warwickshire and Northamptonshire. This family were benefactors to assorted good causes, often associated with the marketing of cheese. On 11 September 1771 the Leicester Infirmary was opened. The principal benefactors were Shuckburgh Ashby, who donated £300, and his grandson Joseph Cradock, who donated £100. The published menu of the meals that the inmates were encouraged to eat shows that cheese was high on the list. Free cheese was provided from the Ashby-run dairies in 1771. The inmates were entitled to three meals a day, one in the morning, one at midday and one in the evening. According

A farmhouse cheese press in the Midlands c.1900.

to the published menu cheese was available for at least one meal per day, amounting to two ounces of cheese per person. This amounted to a full Leicestershire cheese used by the infirmary per week.

The Ashby family had numerous farming tenants in Leicestershire, although because tenancies changed quite frequently it is not possible to name them. One of the most notable landowners whose tenant farmers produced cheese was John Oneby, who was born in Sheepy Magna in 1629 and took up residence at Wykin in 1656, possibly at Wykin Hall, where he was probably the squire. On 11 May 1664 he took up the tenancy of some farmland attached to Quenby Hall. John became the family name over a

The base of a Leicestershire cheese press, retained at Quenby Hall, which was possibly used in the 1760s in the hall's dairy. It was photographed in August 2005.

number of years. On 16 August 1672 Sir John Oneby of Wykin was knighted. A record exists which states that on 9 September 1673 Sir John was involved with cheese dealer Thomas Brown at Mason's Coffee House at Cornhill, London, a centre for the cheese trade in the city. This suggests that the Onebys not only produced cheese, but also transported Leicestershire cheese to numerous trading centres around the country. Through this practice Wykin Hall became one of the major centres for Leicestershire cheese. The Watts family lived in the hall in 1688 and it passed through the female line of the family, to be owned by William Burton in 1774. The following poem was published in 1782:

> From Higham looking down we view
>
> Stoke in the vale below;
>
> And Wykin claims the milking pail,
>
> As plenteous dairies shew;
>
> Hinckley distils the malted grain,
>
> Whence health and vigour flow.

Aston Flamville, January 2008. The dovecote is dated 1745 and was constructed by the Turville family.

In 1790 most of the farming estate of Wykin was held by William Buskerton, with family connections in Leicester, and he factored cheese to the market in the town.

A village with a national reputation for producing fine Leicestershire cheese was Aston Flamville, and in 1720 the enclosure awards came into force in this village. Shuckburgh Ashby purchased the Aston Flamville farm estate in 1746 after it had gained, over the previous 20 years, a reputation for producing excellent cheese from cows grazing in the luxuriant pastures with superior dairies. Aston cheese was considered to be one of the finest on display at the Leicester fairs, but when it was marketed together with Stilton it was the latter which was considered to be the superior cheese. Shuckburgh Ashby became aware of this and wished to produce both types of cheese, so he purchased the Quenby estates near Leicester. The Ashby Flamville estates were run by his grandson, Joseph Cradock. When he died the estate passed to Edmond Cradock Hartopp in 1790.

An entrepreneur, David Wells, purchased the Moat House at Burbage in 1750. In the parkland surrounding this house he raised a fine herd of cows on the superb pastures. He enlarged the dairy and produced and marketed fine Leicestershire cheese. On 1 June 1789 he financed the running of the Whit Monday fair in the marketplace in Hinckley, principally for the promotion of locally produced

Sparkenhoe cheese. This fair had lapsed as an ongoing yearly market since the 1740s. On 6 April 1786 Wells was instrumental in negotiating the first stagecoach run for carrying mail and produce to London. The first postmaster in charge at Hinckley was George Needle. Today Moat House has been demolished and in the park an old peoples' home and a school have been constructed.

A drawing published in 1845 which shows a farmhouse dairy producing Stilton and Leicestershire cheese.

Prior to the middle of the 19th century all of the Sparkenhoe cheese produced in south-west Leicestershire was named after the farmer in question or the hamlet or village. For example, in 1771 Robert Knowles of Nailstone, a farmer with a wide experience of raising cows which were bred to have a very high milk yield, traded in dairy products, including especially fine Nailstone cheese.

An Act of Parliament came into force in 1778, after which the open fields were enclosed at Sapcote. After the enclosures were implemented the rector was no longer required to maintain a bull at his own expense for the use of all the

Wykin Hall c.1790.

Wykin Hall Farm, January 2008.

Kirby Bellars manor house near Melton Mowbray. Pressed and unpressed cheeses were produced at the dairy situated at the house in the 1360s.

farmers in the parish that owned cows. This had been essential to maintain the cycle of calves being born every spring. By 1810 the farmers at Sapcote were noted for the production of fine 'Sapcote Cheese'. They had formed a co-operative under the direction of Revd Thomas Fewin-Turner. Combined, they produced an average of 20 to 30 tons of cheese per year, which retailed in 1810 at 10 pence per pound. This Sapcote cheese was marketed nationally and had a deep orange colour. In the early part of the 19th century, possibly in 1805, Fewin-Turner financed the building of a 'House of Industry' to support the local cheese-producing farmers and to sell all farm products, including butter, wheat, barley

Cheese curd being strained. It would then be tied up and pressed in a linen bag.

and root products. The co-operative supported 202 milking cows, and their products were marketed nationally and into the local markets, principally Leicester.

The open fields around the village of Sutton Cheney were enclosed in 1794. In this enclosure award it was stated that the 'Bull-grass land' must be saved for grass meadows for the grazing of cows to provide milk, in order to produce butter and 'Cheney cheese'. In this Act there is a specific condition that the parish must pay for a bull to be owned for the benefit of the villagers to ensure that calves were born every spring.

One of the most noted farmhouses in England is Donnington-le-Heath manor house. Built in about 1290 as a manor house, it was later let to various tenant farmers. Unfortunately by the 1950s it had become derelict and was used as a pigsty. In 1966 the restoration of the house commenced when Leicestershire County Council purchased the building. Some of the timbers used in 1290 are still incorporated in the building today. It is open throughout the year as a small local museum. Over the centuries the house was owned and occupied by a variety of tenants, who raised cows in the parkland for the production of cheese. After

The House of Industry at Sapcote in 1810. Possibly run by a co-operative, it contained a number of work rooms used for storing wheat, oats, barley and maturing the local farmhouse cheese. The cheese could even have been manufactured on-site. This building was demolished in the 1960s.

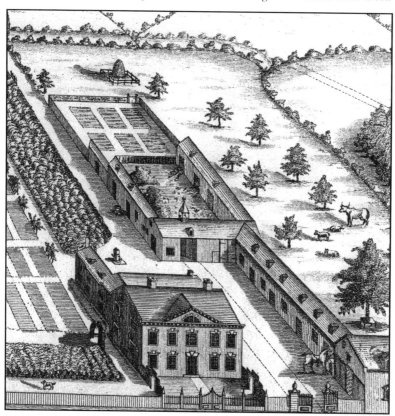

Moat House at Burbage, 1762. This was the home of David Wells, a dealer in fine wine and fine Leicestershire cheese, from 1750 to 1767. The locations of the dairy and cowsheds are indicated by the ventilation duct in the centre of the dairy.

the local enclosure awards, three fields were laid out in the park. In 1801 the manor house was in the ownership of the Burgess family. Two of the tenant farmers were John Dean and Thomas Cheattle. These farmers maintained rich grassland and raised extremely fine cows that produced milk that was converted into fine quality pressed cheese. It is recorded that one of the reasons why this very fine cheese could be produced was because of the quality of water from the deep wells on the site, which contained a degree of salt.

Cheese had been a commodity circulating as a food throughout the Midlands for as long as the farmers had been grazing sheep, obtaining milk and producing a cream cheese there. This cream cheese developed in time into a pressed version. Locally produced cheese was an ideal product to be used as barter, private sale or to be marketed throughout the various weekly village and town markets. It was not until milk yields improved in the 1750s that mass production of cheese commenced. Cheese production expanded throughout the country, farming co-operatives were formed and wealthy landowners organised the tenants to market cheese. Hinckley and Leicester were towns where cheese markets were very well organised. Sparkenhoe cheese was retailed, with the name of the deep orange pressed cheese being taken from manufacturer, village or co-operative. In the 1750s this changed, and two names were awarded to the deep orange pressed cheese: Leicestershire cheese and Leicester cheese. The cheese marketed and sold out of the Leicester markets was identified as Leicester cheese. This resulted in large quantities of pressed cheeses, which were conveyed to the nationally recognised market in Leicester from dairies situated in Warwickshire and Derbyshire, all being labelled Leicester cheese.

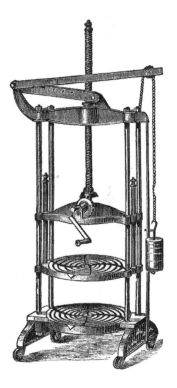

A compound lever-press, dating from 1880, which was used for pressing Leicestershire cheese.

Donington-Le-Heath Manor House, 1795.

Donington-Le-Heath Manor House, June 2008.

In Warwickshire there were a number of individuals factoring cheese into the Leicester market. One of the most noted cheese-makers was John Newdigate Ludford, who lived at Ansley Hall in the village of Ansley, situated west of Nuneaton and to the south-west of Watling Street, near Hinckley. John Ludford inherited the estate after the death of his father in about 1800. By 1811 he had converted the south-west side of the hall into an extensive dairy for cheese-making. With an emphasis on pressed Leicester cheese, he factored cheese to the markets in Leicester.

Cheese production throughout Derbyshire was extensive because of the quality of the water and the splendid meadows of grass, allowing excellent milk to be produced from the fine herds of grazing cows. One of the largest

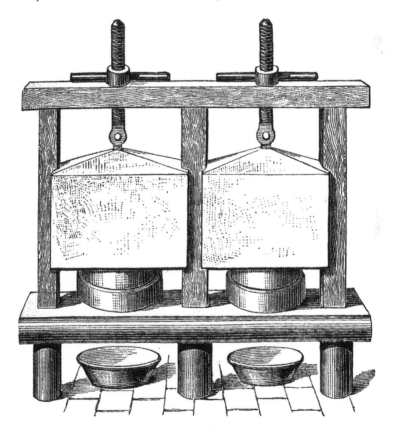

A pair of early 19th-century stone presses. The cheese is pressed in the mould and the whey is collected in two trays beneath.

WILLIAM ADKINSON,

PROVISION MERCHANT,

34, OXFORD STREET, LEICESTER,

WHOLESALE DEPARTMENT, 42A, YORK STREET.

PRIME RIPE BLUE MOULD STILTONS,

OF THE PRESENT SEASON, FROM THE CHOICEST DAIRIES.

FINEST LEICESTERSHIRE, DERBY, AND CHESHIRE CHEESE.

Mild Cured, Smoked, and Plain Breakfast Bacon and Hams.

William Adkinson's advertisement published in 1880. Note he is advertising Stilton, Leicestershire, Derby and Cheshire cheese, with no mention of the so-called 'Leicester cheese'.

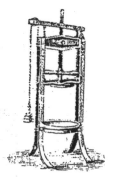

The
KINGSTON
Cheese
Apparatus

For making
Kingston and
other small
Cheeses.

For Prices and particulars apply

VIPAN & HEADLY,

Dairy Engineers, LEICESTER.

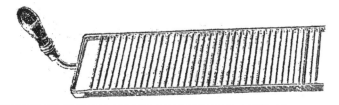

An advertisement published in 1920. Leicestershire was still considered to be an important centre for pressed cheese production.

landowners in 1794 was the third Duke of Devonshire, who lived at Chatsworth House, which was surrounded by extensive parkland. He owned many acres of farmland throughout the county and had many tenant farmers who produced Derbyshire cheese and pressed cheese, which they exported to the large Midlands cheese market in Leicester to be marketed as Leicester cheese. He financed the building of Cavendish Bridge across the River Trent and this carried a trade route leading into the town of Leicester, opening up the Midlands to national trade.

Markets and fairs have been held in various areas of Leicester for over 2,000 years. The Romans ran a market at *Ratae*, and the Danes and Saxons also sold goods in small markets, the first of which were possibly held at the market square that still exists off Gallowtreegate. After the Norman Conquest William I granted the newly appointed Lord of Leicester the right to market goods, and from the late 1060s the Lord or Earl of Leicester controlled and granted the right to hold markets and fairs. The first lord was Hugh de Grantmesnil. In 1199 King John granted the town 'the right to come and go freely to trade through the land with their merchandise'. It is probable that the Wednesday market around the High

Leicestershire and Leicester cheese being collected for distribution by the Midland Railway Co. from the Corn Exchange in the Market Place, Leicester, May 1911.

Holstein-Friesian cows waiting to be milked at Sparkenhoe Farm in November 2007.

Cross, for the sale of butter and eggs, was founded at this time. Butter is a very loose term, as it also refers to soft cream cheese such as slipcoat. The Saturday market is mentioned in a deed of 1298.

In 1360, during the last years of Henry, Duke of Lancaster, the mayor and burgesses of Leicester were given the right to control the running of the markets. In 1473 King Edward IV confirmed the terms for the running of a market, which was initially granted in 1360. Although subject to some alterations over the centuries, the rights of the people of Leicester to run a market are still maintained.

In 1748 the Exchange was built in Market Place and it became the centre for marketing Leicester, Leicestershire and Stilton cheese in 1750. Cheese factors purchased a wide variety of cheese for distribution from the exchange and for sale in the speciality markets and fairs on a daily basis. Pressed cheese was available throughout the year, and unpressed cheese, in particular Stilton cheese, became available during the autumn months when the speciality cheese fairs were held.

In the early part of the 19th century changes in the production of cheese occurred due to the impact of the Industrial Revolution, as the demand for cheese as a food increased.

The marketing of cheese expanded throughout the British Isles. Improvements in agricultural techniques were a contributing factor. The fenlands of Lincolnshire, Huntingdonshire and Cambridgeshire were being drained, which meant that the production of wheat, barley and oats increased. Trading in agricultural produce increased, as did methods of marketing the farmers' products. Two trading halls were built in nearby Grantham in 1852, situated very close to the Great North Road, the most important highway built in England for over 1,000 years. One of the halls that took precedence was the Corn Exchange, and this was controlled by a co-operative. It marketed corn and other agricultural products including butter, Stilton and Leicester cheese.

A Sparkenhoe Red Leicestershire cheese positioned on top of a 19th-century cheese press stone, at Sparkenhoe Farm at Upton, 2007.

Sparkenhoe Red Leicestershire cheese maturing in the farmhouse dairy.

David Clarke with a Sparkenhoe Red Leicestershire cheese at the entrance to his dairy, November 2007. This dairy markets its cheese as Sparkenhoe Red Leicester Cheese.

The Market Place, Leicester, 1840. The open area of this ancient town could have held markets during the Roman occupation and for the next 1,000 years. The Exchange, centre left, was built in 1748, on what was originally the site of the magistrates' court and prison cells. The Exchange was demolished and the present Corn Exchange was built on the existing site in 1850, to a design by William Flint.

Chapter Three
The Cheese Wars

*A*rise in prices engendered by the French Revolution and the eventual war with France meant expensive food in Great Britain. Through the next decade the prices of corn, meat and particularly cheese rose dramatically. By means of marketing farm-produced commodities in the Midlands, landlords became very prosperous; they doubled their rents on tenant farmers, who in turn increased the price of the produce they sold in the local markets. Grazing of cattle for the production of meat and dairy produce ensured that the local farmers and dealers prospered, though not as much as the arable farmers, as the price of wheat rose year on year from 43 shillings a quarter to 126 shillings a quarter. The price of bread made life very difficult for the lowly paid workers living and working in the urban areas of industrial towns such as Leicester, as bread and cheap cheese provided sustenance to the industrial workforce.

This all came to a head in September 1766 when a large group of hosiery workers assembled in the marketplace in the centre of Hinckley and attacked the wagons that were in the process of distributing cheese for sale at the Monday market. There must have been some form of forward planning, and those wagons that escaped the mob in Hinckley were ambushed on the main street of Earl Shilton, where the wagons were stopped on the way to the Leicester market and all the cheese was distributed throughout the village.

During Tuesday in the last week of September 1766 Charles Pridmore, a cheese factor operating out of Market Harborough, dealing in large quantities of cheese to be sold in street markets on Humberstone Gate and out of the Exchange in Leicester market, was carrying cheese to Leicester. He obtained cheese from farmers near Quenby Hall and others producing farmhouse cheeses north of Market Harborough. There was a large warehouse at the rear of the Bell Hotel on Humberstone Gate, and the cheese he stored in this warehouse was sold on the wide highway outside this hotel on a daily basis. A variety of cheese was sold – mainly Leicestershire pressed cheese and, during the autumn months, Stilton cheese. The autumn fair was due to take place in October, by which time prices of cheese had increased and very little was available for local consumption. This led to disquiet throughout the town and the county concerning the price of cheese, and it was obvious that cheese factors were controlling the price of cheese in Leicestershire. Because of riots in and around Hinckley earlier in the month, magistrates were attempting to control the marketing of cheese. The local courts were unaware that large quantities of cheese were being stored and sold at the Bell Hotel, not under the control of the Exchange in the marketplace. After the incident at Hinckley, Pridmore became alarmed and loaded up a wagon with cheese stored at the Bell. While attempting to leave the town via Humberstone Gate the wagon was stopped by a large group of women, who climbed into the vehicle and distributed the cheese to the large crowd that had gathered. The mob then marched down Humberstone Gate to the Bell Hotel, forced open the doors

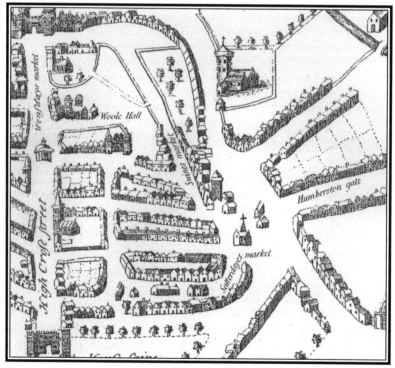

The layout of the centre of Leicester, c.1600. The map indicates the three markets and the sites of the numerous fairs.

The Exchange, Leicester, 1796. On this engraving a covered wagon containing cheese is waiting to be unloaded. The cheese was in the vaults.

to the warehouse and began distributing the cheese in relays to the large gathering of local people. It is obvious that again there was forward planning. As soon as the warehouse doors had been broken down a representative of the local magistrates arrived with Ensign Mortimer from the 17th of Foot, 'he beat the drums-to-arms' and the next instant a platoon of soldiers formed into a square with fixed bayonets, marched forward and forced the mob to retreat from the Bell Hotel. Twenty minutes later the whole regiment arrived and attempted to clear Humberstone Gate. The officer in charge read out the Riot Act and in response the large crowd of people formed a solid mass at the end of Humberstone Gate, facing the fixed bayonets of a regiment of troops. At this point the magistrates intervened to prevent considerable loss of life, and, under guard, wagons were brought forward and the remaining cheese was transported to the Exchange in the marketplace. The mayor addressed the crowd that had followed the defended wagons and ordered them to disperse. He stated that he would allow the populace to purchase cheese in the market the following day under controlled distribution at 2d per pound. He then placed troops with fixed bayonets in position in front of the Exchange. However, the locals were aware that many inns throughout the centre of Leicester stored Leicester cheese, as the large flat cheese was easily rolled

A painting produced in the late 18th century showing the marketplace in Leicester at the time of the Cheese Wars of 1766. Two troopers are on guard in front of the Exchange.

from inn to inn and was popular with the population. The mob dispersed from the guarded Exchange and began visiting some of the inns. In the chaos, much cheese was stolen. Wherever possible, platoons of soldiers organised for some of the cheese stored in isolated inns to be transported to the Exchange for safe-keeping. A platoon of troops was stationed in the Market Square and the rest of the regiment was dismissed.

Leicester was the centre for the cheese trade, and with the October cheese fair drawing close wagonloads of cheese were being conveyed to the Exchange after dark; wagons from Burton upon Trent, Ashby-de-la-Zouch and farms in Derbyshire, which were all loaded with pressed cheese, were held outside the town. Organisers of the mob were well aware of this when the convoy of wagons arrived at Coal Hill (now the Clock Tower). Just after eight o'clock, the riotous mob (some 4,000 people) charged the wagons and stole the cheese. Again the drums were sounded, and belatedly the local regiment of soldiers charged the mob with fixed bayonets. 'Carnage took place', and flaming projectiles were thrown at the troops as they advanced behind their bayonets. It has never been recorded how many people died from bayonet wounds.

The troops managed to save one of the three wagons from plunder. This was the Derbyshire wagon, containing Leicester cheese, and it was conveyed under guard to the Exchange, unloaded and placed under armed guard. At 11 o'clock that night the mob dispersed to the entrance of the town, hoping that further wagons of cheese would arrive. On the following morning, just before midday, a quantity of cheese was offered for sale from the Exchange for 2d per lb. Four local women attacked the magistrates and were arrested and dragged to the local jail, where considerable violence took place before one of the women was released by the mob. At nine o'clock in the evening a riotous mob attacked the prison, troops were called and five ringleaders were arrested and placed in the cells. On Thursday a guard of 100 mounted troops surrounded the prison and were each issued with 15 rounds of balls and gunpowder, with instructions to open fire if attacked. The town crier addressed the mob, instructing them to disperse, and eventually peace was restored. Some of those arrested during the riot were held in prison until March 1767, when they were all fined. If they could not pay this sum, however, they were deported. The Leicester cheese riots were not over; the riotous mob decided that the open countryside was a more convenient area in which to attack incoming wagons.

Leicester cheese from Derbyshire was one of the largest imports to the city markets. It was mainly produced on the farms owned by the Duke of Devonshire, who lived at Chatsworth House. The third Duke of Devonshire had funded the building of Cavendish Bridge, which crossed the River Trent north of Castle Donington in the 18th century. Named after Lord Charles Cavendish, the younger brother of the third Duke, this was built as a much easier method of carrying sheep, wool and cheese to the large Leicester markets than by ferry. Lord Cavendish controlled the bridge, and any person walking across the bridge was charged a penny, while a wagon was

A Leicestershire soldier billeted in Leicester, c.1760.

charged half a crown. The Devonshire family travelled across the bridge free of charge. To avoid the Leicester traders having to pay a fee for crossing the bridge from Derbyshire, a warehouse was built on the north side of the bridge to store wool, corn and cheese. On the Sunday which followed the Leicester cheese riots, an organised group of individuals marched on Cavendish Bridge and attacked

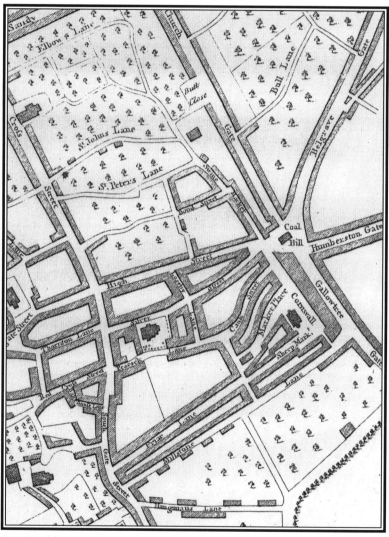

A section of the very accurate plan of the centre of Leicester drawn and published by John Prior of Ashby-de-la-Zouch in 1777. The Exchange is situated opposite the Cornwall in the Market Place.

Chatsworth House, Derbyshire, c.1850.

Chatsworth House, Derbyshire, with cows, c.1920.

The remains of the footway that was built across Cavendish Bridge from the Leicestershire side, opposite the Old Crown Inn, April 2008.

the fortified warehouse, firing ball and grapeshot in a controlled attack. The defenders within the warehouse held off the siege by returning fire with muskets and fowling pieces. Throughout the night the defenders held their position. After dusk the attackers built positions on the bridge, prior to a main attack planned for first light the following morning. Before the attackers could charge they were assailed from the front and rear simultaneously by over 30 mounted horsemen, farmers and footmen from Chatsworth House, possibly assisted by local Derbyshire militia. The attackers were armed with swords and pistols, and the mob was routed. There is no record of who was killed or arrested during this skirmish at Cavendish Bridge. Shortly after the confrontation the toll for crossing the bridge was reduced. This meant that there was no charge for people on foot, but a chaise was charged 6d and a wagon of four horses 10d (Cavendish Bridge was destroyed in the disastrous floods during the spring of 1947). There must have been a number of deaths after the battle at Cavendish Bridge, but there is no record of any other incident of violence attributed to 'the Cheese Wars'.

Cavendish Bridge in the 1920s. It was destroyed during the floods of 1947.

An engraving of Cavendish Bridge, 1794. On this bridge a minor battle took place in 1766, involving individuals from Leicestershire attacking a warehouse defended by estate workers from the Chatsworth estate in Derbyshire.

The Old Crown Inn at Cavendish Bridge on the Leicestershire bank of the River Trent, April 2008. It is an 18th-century public house that was built after the 'Cheese Wars' of 1766.

The tolls at Cavendish Bridge. During the time of the 'Cheese Wars' in the 18th century this plaque was positioned at the approach to the bridge. Today it has been restored and erected on the Derbyshire side of the River Trent.

Chapter Four

Red Leicester

The cheese of Leicestershire was traditionally a pressed cheese, a crumbly cheese with a unique taste produced in the rolling countryside of south-west Leicestershire known as the Sparkenhoe Hundred. At a very early date this pressed cheese took precedence over the soft cream cheese made in the area, although this type of unpressed cream cheese continued to be produced in east Leicestershire in the Framland Hundred.

Colouring of the pressed cheese was essential, and this was done using a vegetable rennet obtained from Lady's Bedstraw. The yellow flowers, the stalks and leaves provided the rennet, while the roots, when boiled, provided a red dye. It was this plant which provided the deep orange-red cheese that has famously been the cheese of Leicestershire.

After the Battle of Waterloo, when the Duke of Wellington finally beat Napoleon and the French army, Great Britain entered a golden age. World trade expanded and Great Britain certainly 'ruled the waves'! One of Britain's allies in the Peninsular War was Portugal, after Wellington drove the French army out of Portugal. A friendly arrangement through trade between the two countries developed. Part of the Portuguese empire was the vast country of Brazil, and imports into England from South America expanded via Portuguese trading systems that were ratified in 1826. Dyed cloth was one of the many goods imported, and one of the red dyes in use was annatto. It was imported into England in cake form and was then ground down and used as a bright deep orange-red dye. Unlike some of the other vegetable dyes it was non-poisonous, and it was used, alongside animal rennet, in the production of Leicester cheese.

In 1837 Queen Victoria came to the throne at the head of a large Empire, and as the great leaps forward in industrial expansion commenced, the production of cheese as a reliable food for the working masses was essential. A large proportion of the farmers in the Sparkenhoe Hundred raised cows, produced milk and converted this into cheese throughout the year. Nationally, identifying speciality cheese was essential for the agents and factors involved with the selling of these highly marketable varieties. At the time Cheddar cheese was the main speciality cheese of England, produced throughout the UK (and in the US) with a rich orange colour. In order to compete with Cheddar, the cheese factors dominating the Leicester cheese trade decided that they needed a distinctive Leicester cheese.

In the 1840s the use of a rennet using annatto combined with the rumen of an unweaned calf became widespread. Many traditional farmers around Hinckley continued to use Lady's Bedstraw as the coagulating agent, but the large-scale producers of Leicester cheese used annatto and animal rennet. Until the outbreak of World War One in 1914 there were two varieties of cheese in the Midlands: Leicestershire cheese and Leicester cheese, with the Leicestershire cheese lighter in colour. The red-coloured Leicester was produced in Derbyshire and Warwickshire and spread down into Somerset and through other counties, and was eventually produced as a red-dyed cheese in the US and the British colonies. It was a different pressed cheese to those that were produced in south-west Leicestershire. After World War Two this red-coloured cheese was marketed as Red Leicester and its popularity soared.

After World War One all the cheese producers of pressed cheese, including the small farmers, used annatto as the colouring agent. However, during World War Two annatto was banned as a colouring agent because it was a non-essential but expensive import, and all pressed cheeses that were produced were yellow in colour, similar to Cheddar cheese. As they were no longer producing unique cheese, this spelled the end for cheese-producing farms in the Sparkenhoe Hundred. One farmer who survived was Robert Shepherd, who began farming in Bagworth Farm Park in 1922 and was producing Leicester cheese until the outbreak of World War Two. During and after the conflict he then marketed milk and produced a small amount of pressed cheese. In 1948 he started producing Red Leicester cheese, but he and his family could not compete with the mass production dairies and national bureaucracy, and his farm ceased cheese production in 1956.

After World War Two a few of the dairy farmers who were marketing cheese made a few pressed cheeses from their surplus milk and this cheese was sold locally. However, it gained little or no support and by 1960 no pressed cheese was produced by farmers in west Leicestershire because of the restrictions imposed on their dairies by the Milk Marketing Board.

The growth of Leicestershire and Leicester cheese took a major step forward after the Industrial Revolution and the ending of the French wars, and this slowly brought about the start of private ownership of land. In 1815 the Corn Laws were passed. William IV became king in 1830 and obtained considerable respect from the people. His reign was memorable because the Reform Act and the Poor Laws were passed through Parliament. The Act and Poor Laws which William IV introduced dramatically changed the power base in agriculture, as wealthy landowners lost power and private individuals gained control and respect through trade. Cheese was by that time an important part of the Leicestershire economy and cheese factors became important figures in the marketing of cheese. At first they purchased cheese and placed it in store to mature, specifically for sale in the local cheese fairs. Cheese was then purchased in bulk from these middle men for retailing in London. In 1835 very large cheese fairs were held in Hinckley on 26 August and Leicester on 10 October and 8 December, and these were held in the town Market Square. The cheese dealers who were factoring cheese in Leicester in 1834 were: John Atkins, Humberstone Gate; John Austin, Haymarket; Robert Coleman, Belgrave Gate; William Robson Humphrey, Cheapside; John Eamer Marshal, Horse Fair Street; Joseph Sharpe, Humberstone Gate; William Smith & Son, High Street. Samuel Rubley was dealing in cheese in 1835 at Stoke Golding.

In 1846, 10 years after Queen Victoria was crowned, cheese factoring in Leicester had expanded, with the following being prominent factors at the time: John Austin, Rutland Street; Charles Charlton, 43 & 45 Gallowtree Gate; R.J. Freeman, Market Place; John Manning, High Street and South Bond Street; John Marshall, Horsefair Street; J. and T. Nunnely, High Cross Street; Charles Pratt, Newarke Street; Loes and Roberts, Market Place and Hotel Street; William Scampton, High Street; Paddy and Swain, High Cross Street; George Willey, 38 Granby Street. During the same year two cheese factors were operating out of Lutterworth: John Earton and John Stiles on High Street.

In 1849 11 cheese fairs were held in Leicester, which also marketed farm livestock including sheep, cattle and pigs. Leicestershire, Leicester and Stilton cheese was on offer. These fairs were held simultaneously in Market Place and on Humberstone Gate on: 4 January, 2 March, the Saturday after Easter Monday, 12 May, 1 June, 5 July, 1 August, 13 September, 10 October, 2 November and 8 December. In 1849, six of the traders who had been factoring in 1846 were still in business. These were: Austin, Belvoir Street; Walter Marshall, Haymarket;

Samuel Mather, Welford Road; Samuel Riley, Bedford Street; Roberts and Lees, Market Place; Russell and Sheen, Bridge Street. Joseph Burdett was factoring in cheese at Desford, and four cheese factors had begun dealing out of Hinckley: John Argile, Market Place; William Berridge, Castle Street; William Gutteridge, Lower Bond Street and Joseph Spencer, Castle Street.

The Market Place in Hinckley became the centre for very large cheese fairs by 1862 and in that year they were held on 26 August and 10 November. These fairs specialised in Sparkenhoe Leicestershire, a red pressed cheese. In the same year two large cheese fairs were held in Market Place and on Humberstone Gate in Leicester, specialising in Stilton and Leicester cheese. Some of this cheese was factored out of the warehouse at the rear of the Bell Hotel, owned by Arthur Boyer, 26 Humberstone Gate, in 1862. At 153 Belgrave Gate in Leicester, John Belton ran the Old Cheese public house and marketed a true Leicestershire cheese, which was deep orange in colour and not coloured by the imported red dye annatto.

Eventually the number of cheese factors in Leicester reduced, although the ones which remained still marketed three types of local cheese. Six factors who remained included: Evans and Stafford, Campbell Street; Tebbit & Roberts, Market Place; John Hardyman, 5 Victoria Parade; Samuel Mather, 65 Market Place; George Sheen, 21, 23 & 25 West Bridge; William Wells, 8 Union Street. These six agents were still operating in Leicester and were joined by seven more cheese traders marketing both Leicester and Stilton cheese. One of the most important was Horatio Emberlin, 18 Gallowtree Gate, who specialised in marketing Stilton cheese. The demand for Stilton cheese that was produced in Leicestershire and Rutland was taking over from the demand for traditionally produced Leicester cheese. Red-coloured cheese remained popular, however, and was now being produced in many of the large dairies situated throughout Somerset and the West Country, all marketed as Leicester cheese.

On 4 May 1870 the first purpose-built cheese factory was opened in Derbyshire for the production of pressed cheese. The first Longford Dairy could not meet the demand and so a second dairy was built 10 miles away. This vast dairy complex produced a wide range of pressed cheese and also exported Leicester cheese. In the first published accounts for a 12-month period the dairy spent approximately £12 on annatto and £50 on rennet skins. The total sale of all cheeses in 12 months amounted to 2,200 cwt, and income from sales was £8,000.

In 1875 Thomas Nuttall realised the marketing of true Leicester cheese was in decline because of the large national competitors, who were all selling their cheeses under the name of Leicester. From a farming family, he had an interest in Leicestershire cheeses and so he developed the first factory producing Stilton cheeses. He took over a disused Leicester cheese factory at the Manor House, Beeby, near Leicester, in 1875 and adapted it to produce factory-made Stilton cheese. He employed 30 people and purchased milk from farmers in the surrounding villages. Before 1875, all Stilton cheese was made in farmhouse dairies from the farm's own milk and was a seasonal product. By establishing a factory for the mass manufacture of this once seasonal cheese Thomas Nuttall changed the industry forever. He soon had his competitors, however, as many local farmers decided they could convert their milk into Stilton cheese rather than continue to make Leicester cheese.

The Sparkenhoe Hundred to the west of Leicester was still operational at this time and traditional Leicestershire cheese continued to be produced in the area. In 1847 the East Coast railway line into London opened up and the amount of cheese being produced increased; particularly the amount of Stilton, which already had a ready market in the capital. Farmers in the north of the county, over into Rutland and around Market Harborough, dismantled their presses, purchased Stilton cheese hoops and expanded into the growing Stilton cheese trade.

All of the cheese factors in Leicester soon began marketing both Stilton and Red Leicester cheese. By 1877 there were nine factors of cheese in Leicester. These included Horatio Emberlin, who was operating out of the Exchange in Market Place and who was maturing Stilton cheese in the basement and offering rounds of Leicester cheese from his general store. Robert Adkinson, a large retailer of cheese and assorted groceries, with shops and warehouses on Hotel Street and Belgrave Gate, opened for business in 1876. Twenty-two years later he was operating out of Stilton House, 10 & 12 Hotel Street, near the Market Place. In an advertisement published in 1898 he stated that he had purchased Stilton and Leicestershire cheese made in the county from several dairies and made the recommendation that they were far superior to what was offered by most houses in the local trade. Thomas Bond, a cheese factor dealing only in Leicestershire cheese, was operating in Upper Castle Street, Hinckley, in 1877. Three years later, John Payne was wholesaling Leicestershire cheese in 10 New Building at

Hinckley. The marketing of Leicestershire-produced cheeses was spreading very quickly throughout the Midlands at this time.

After a survey conducted in 1880 it was found that there were numerous small farms running dairies around Hinckley and Market Bosworth, and one of the largest was run by John Davis, who operated out of Wykin Hall. It is now very difficult to class whether a cheese was Leicester cheese or Leicestershire cheese from the records that survive, but it is thought that at that time Leicester cheese was red and Leicestershire cheese was orange. The main dye would have been annatto, although it was possible that some of the traditional dairy farmers still produced 'old' Leicestershire cheese using Lady's Bedstraw as the rennet and dye.

In the hamlet of Upton, Henry Taverner gained a national reputation with his herd of 20 Longhorns. One of his cows produced '16 quarts of milk' when milked. In his dairy he produced four and a half tons of Leicestershire cheese per season.

In 1880 there was a conflict of interest in marketing cheese out of Leicester, and the two leading factors were Robert Adkinson and William Adkinson. Robert was the largest commercial dealer, operating out of Stilton House, marketing

A mould used in the manufacture of pressed Leicester cheese in the 1940s at Scalford dairy. In 1940 all dairies were banned from producing Stilton cheese, so Scalford proceeded to produce Red Leicester cheese. Central government then banned the use of annatto, so they attempted to produce a type of Cheddar cheese. They could not compete with the large national dairies, however, and eventually they closed the dairy down for the duration of World War Two.

Leicester cheese, while William worked with a wholesale department at 34 Oxford Street and sold Leicestershire cheese. Eighteen years later Robert was concentrating his efforts on his finest Leicestershire cheese, which suggests that the national trade in the red-coloured Leicester cheese was affecting the local market. From 1900 onwards the amount of cheese being factored from Leicester on a weekly basis deteriorated and the industry was only briefly revived at the cheese fairs that were held in the spring and autumn. However, even these closed down before World War One.

In the decade before World War One, three specialist farmers dealing in cheese were in business at Acton Flamville. There were six dairy farms at Wykin. The main agent for local Leicestershire cheese in Hinckley was Stephen Henry Pilgrim, the High Bailiff, who was operating in Castle Street. It is believed that he attempted to form a Leicestershire Cheese Association at about this time. Unfortunately, now that Stilton cheese was the major cheese coming from Leicestershire, it dominated the market and the factoring of cheese out of the county.

World War One affected the industry and cheese was produced and marketed on an ad hoc basis. Labour was in short supply, and this affected the small Leicestershire cheese farmers. Some farm workers survived the Western Front and after the Armistice went back to assist the dairy farmers. Despite the shortage of workers the dairy farms opened up again and traded with remaining factors operating out of Leicester, including Robert Adkinson. In 1922 Robert Shepherd became one of the leading Leicester cheese producers from his dairy farm at Bagworth. Richard Wathes at Castle Farm, Kirby Muxloe, was producing Leicester cheese and R. Wathes & Son were trading as cheese factors out of Nos 98 to 100 King Richard Road, Leicester. Callow Park Dairy were running the Central Cheese Factory on Church Street, Leicester, producing Leicester cheese and a commercial cheese using a different recipe to the traditional Leicestershire. Their warehouse was situated at Nos 23 to 25 Wharf Street.

Between the wars in the 1930s there were 11 registered cheese-makers who were commercially producing cheese on factory lines, and there were also many small farmers producing a variety of cheese from their surplus milk during the summer months. Some dairies produced Leicester cheese when the demand arose, while continuing to produce Stilton. In 1936 Leicester Creameries Ltd were producing Leicester cheese and selling it from a property at No. 167 Western Road, Leicester.

In 1939 World War Two broke out, and during the winter of 1940–41 the British Government placed a ban on the production of Stilton cheese and the use of annatto. Some of the dairies therefore attempted to produce a pressed cheese similar to Cheddar. A number of dairies closed as a result of the financial and production restrictions and never reopened. This sounded the death knell for the production of pressed cheese in Leicestershire. Nationally, Red Leicester cheese was produced in large quantities in Melton Mowbray, and Tuxford & Tebbutts on Thorpe Road expanded their Stilton cheese production, although they could not match the price of the large national producers.

The deep orange 'true' Leicestershire cheese continued to be produced, however, and the practice continues to this day in dairies situated in the rich grassy pastures in the rolling countryside around the town of Hinckley in the area once known as the Sparkenhoe Hundred. The ancient ridge and furrow pastures where rushes grow in the furrows are considered to be among the finest meadows for grazing, especially if they have not been ploughed for centuries. Cows grazing in these fields produce the creamy milk that is so necessary to produce a splendid cheese. The finest Leicestershire pressed cheese should be deep orange in colour and must be allowed to mature for 12 months. The flavour must be rich, full and nutty, and the texture a little flaky and moist when cut. This is as opposed to the mass-produced Red Leicester cheese that is deep red, waxy and rubbery in texture.

In November 2005 David and Jo Clarke began making cheese from Sparkenhoe Farm in the hamlet of Upton, approximately five miles to the north-west of Hinckley, three miles from Watling Street, in the rich meadows where pressed Leicestershire cheese has been made for over 1,000 years. George Chapman was making Leicestershire cheese at Sparkenhoe Farm in 1745, but his family stopped producing cheese in 1875 as they could not compete with the national factory dairies. The Clarke family have lived in this area of the Sparkenhoe Hundred for many generations, and today David manages a herd of 150 pedigree Holstein Friesian cows. They graze ancient grassy pastures, and calving takes place continuously to ensure that the milk supply is as consistent as possible. The unpasteurised milk is pumped from the milking parlour directly into the cheese vat. Then animal rennet and annatto is added, the milk coagulates, the curds and whey separate and some whey is drained off. The remaining curds and whey are then gently scalded, which separates the curds, which are then cut into blocks and turned to release further whey. The curds are then broken down by passing them through a curd mill, after which salt is added. The salted curds are then placed in moulds to set.

In the Clarkes' dairy there are two sizes of mould capable of producing the traditional wheels. There is a large size, where the cheese weighs 20kg, and a standard size, which weighs 10kg. The cheese is pressed for 24 hours, after which it is turned and pressed for a further 24 hours. The pressed cheese is then wrapped in fine linen and has lard rubbed into its surface. The cheese is then stacked on wooden shelves in the maturing room for four and a half months, at a constant temperature of 10 degrees.

Before the Clarkes began production it had been 50 years since any farmer had made the traditional Leicestershire cheese in the area. Sparkenhoe Red Leicester cheese is produced by the Leicestershire Handmade Cheese Company, at Upton, and the directors are David and Jo Clarke. Ironically, although the company produces 'true' Leicestershire cheese, the postal address of this farmhouse dairy is: Handmade Cheese Co., Sparkenhoe Farm, Main Road, Upton, Nuneaton, Warwickshire!

Long Clawson Dairy, near Melton Mowbray, are manufacturing a factory-produced aged Leicestershire red cheese from pasteurised milk. It is on sale in the Melton Cheeseboard, run by Tim Brown in Melton Mowbray.

Farmhouse Red Leicester cheese has also been made in the traditional manner in Devon. Quicke's Red Leicester, owned by J.G. Quicke in Exeter, Devon, produces a dark red-coloured russet from pasteurised milk. In Cheshire, Overton Hall's Red Leicester is made by Mr and Mrs Barnet at Overton Hall, Cheshire. The cheese is a flat millstone-shaped cheese, cloth bound and waxed and made using pasteurised milk with vegetable rennet.

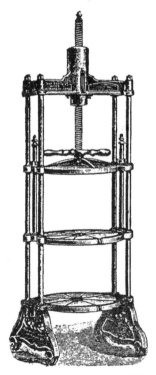

A standard cheese press, c.1870.

The Corn Exchange, built in 1850 by William Flint, as it looked in 1903. In the 18th and 19th centuries the town of Leicester was the East Midlands' centre for the sale of cheese. Cheese was the main food marketed from the Exchange, along with wheat, barley and oats.

The Fair on Humberstone Gate. The Bell Hotel is on the left, c.1900.

Gallowtree Gate, c.1920. In 1860 Horatio Emberlin was factoring and selling cheese from his grocer's shop at No. 18 Gallowtree Gate, Leicester.

VICCARS COLLYER,

Wholesale Provision Merchant,

IMPORTER OF

OSTEND, FRENCH, AND IRISH BUTTERS, AMERICAN CHEESE, &c.

HOME-CURED HAMS AND BACON.

LARD IN TINS, KEGS, AND BLADDERS.

LEICESTER AND STILTON CHEESE.

24, SILVER STREET, LEICESTER,

HALF A MINUTE'S WALK FROM THE CLOCK TOWER.

CENTRAL HALL, SILVER STREET, for LECTURES, &c., for Terms apply to Mr. Collyer.

An 1880 advertisement for Viccars Collyer, a leading promoter of international food, especially cheese.

Corn Exchange,

The Corn Exchange on Westgate in Grantham, which was erected in 1852 to cater for the expanding corn trade that resulted from the draining of the Lincolnshire Fen. Situated at the side of the Great North Road, it also became a centre for the marketing of Stilton and Leicester cheese.

A wood engraving of the Longford Factory in Derbyshire, 1870. This dairy produced large quantities of pressed cheese, especially a deep orange-red cheese that was delivered to the Leicester markets to be sold as Leicester cheese.

R. L. ADKINSON,

"STILTON HOUSE,"

10 & 12, HOTEL STREET, LEICESTER.

PRIME RIPE BLUE MOULD STILTONS,

OF THE PRESENT SEASON, FROM THE CHOICEST DAIRIES.

FINEST CHEDDAR, LEICESTER, CHESHIRE, & AMERICAN CHEESE.

R. L. A. calls special attention to his NORMANDY, BRITTANY, and DEVONSHIRE BUTTERS, for which he has made arrangements for fresh supplies every week.

MILD-CURED, SMOKED, AND PLAIN BREAKFAST BACON AND HAMS.

EGGS FROM THE COUNTRY TWICE A WEEK.

FARMERS SUPPLIED WITH CHEESE COLOURING SKINS.

This is a very interesting advertisement, published in 1880 by Richard Adkinson. He was a national retailer factoring large quantities of cheese. He supplied the local trade with imported calves' rumens – salted 'vels', dyed with annatto. These were then soaked in warm water to produce coloured rennet, which was used in the manufacture of Leicester cheese.

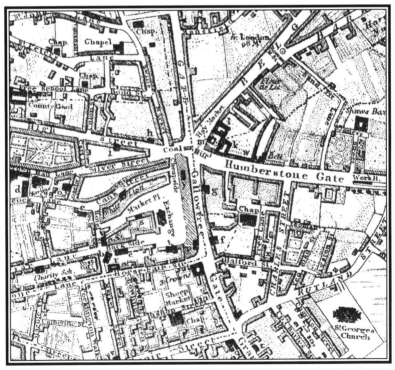

An extract from A. Cockshow's map of 1828, which indicates the Haymarket; Market Place and the Exchange; Horsefair Street; the Sheep Market and the Bell Hotel on Humberstone Gate.

The extensive dairies and brewhouse to the south-west of Ansley Hall, Warwickshire, which was owned by John Newdigate Ludford in 1811. Note the ventilation duct in the centre of the maturing room of the main dairy.

Ansley Hall, April 2008. Originally a cheese dairy, it is now a private house, the home of the Morewood family.

Pedigree Holstein-Friesian cows grazing in the lush meadows in Upton, June 2008.

Holstein cows feeding at Sparkenhoe Farm in Upton, June 2008.

David Clarke and David Chevell checking the separation of the curd from the whey in the cheese-making vats in the dairy at Sparkenhoe Farm, Upton, June 2008.

Breaking up the cheese curd in the dairy at Sparkenhoe Farm, June 2008.

Jenny Summers preparing the cheese moulds to be filled with the prepared curds, June 2008.

David Chevell filling the cheese moulds for stacking into the cheese presses, June 2008.

The cheese press at Sparkenhoe Farm being filled with cheese moulds by David Clarke, June 2008.

Sparkenhoe cheese, which matures for four and a half months on wooden shelves.

Cutting the matured cheese in the traditional method with a special knife at the Sparkenhoe dairy, June 2008.

Jo Shimkus cutting Sparkenhoe Red Leicester cheese on sale in Neal's Yard Dairy at Borough Market near London Bridge, October 2008.

Tim Brown at the Melton Cheeseboard, 8 Windsor Street, Melton Mowbray, Leicestershire. A wide variety of cheeses are offered from this shop, which specialises in Stilton and Red Leicestershire cheese. Tim is holding half of a Stilton cheese.

Red Leicestershire cheese, manufactured by Long Clawson Dairy from pasteurised milk, is on offer at the Melton Cheeseboard, along with Sparkenhoe cheese.

Chapter Five

Stilton Cheese

S tilton Cheese is considered to be the finest cheese ever developed in England and is enjoyed by millions of people worldwide. The village of Stilton sits on Ermine Street (the Great North Road), a highway constructed by the Romans, possibly along the line of a prehistoric trackway which skirted the marshes of eastern England. Long-distance routes such as the Great North Road needed centres for supplying the needs of weary travellers. Stilton (Stichiltone) was such a place, sited about 70 miles from London, a day's journey on horseback or by hard-driven coach. The Romans constructed a trading centre off Ermine Street, and no doubt the fast chariots of Imperial Rome carrying messages to the troop commander on Hadrian's Wall passed this way in the first and second centuries AD and stopped for refreshment. In the spring of 2006 a complete Roman cheese mould was found on the site of this camp. This mould was used in the production of lightly moulded cream cheese.

After the fall of the Roman Empire and during the colonization of England by the Saxons, Danes and Norman invaders, who also produced cheese in Stichiltone, the roadway of Ermine Street continued to be the most important highway in England.

In the first detailed map showing the main highways of England, published in 1675 by John Ogilby, Stilton is depicted as a substantial centre on the Great North Road, consisting of two long, stoutly constructed rows of buildings, one on each side of the highway. Records indicate that many inns existed in Stilton, which were controlled by various religious houses before the dissolution of the monasteries. One example of such an establishment is the Blue Bell Inn, which was being run by Edward Tebald in 1501. The village soon became a centre for trade, which presumably included the sale of cream cheese, a variety of which was made locally. Pressed cheese was imported to Stilton along with cream cheese produced on the Berkeley estate at Wymondham. A pressed cheese took eight to nine months to mature and the white cream cheese was edible after two weeks

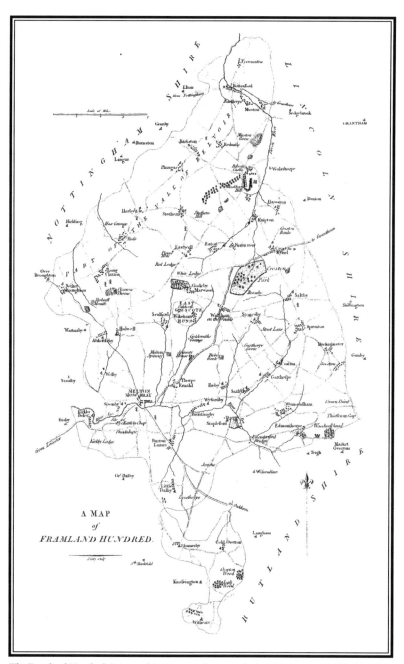

The Framland Hundred, Leicestershire, a cream cheese-producing district, engraved by John Cary in 1810. Wymondham is situated in the south-east corner of this map.

and matured by 12 weeks. The estate specialised in the raising of cows for milk and cheese production. The Great North Road was less than two miles away, and the town of Stilton was situated a few miles down Ermine Street.

Cheese was made in the hamlets surrounding the small town of Stilton from Roman times up until the 1780s. The speciality cheese that became known as Stilton cheese is a soft cheese that develops blue veins as it ages. An original recipe used in and around Stilton made cheese from ewes', goats' and cows' milk. Ten

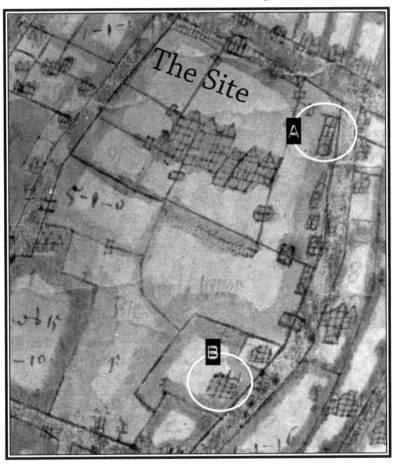

An extract of the Sedley Estate map of 1652. The manor house is indicated as 'The Site'. The manor house's dairy (A) is situated on the top left-hand corner on the road junction and pre-dates this map. In this dairy the Berkeleys produced a cream cheese that developed blue veins as it aged. Below the manor house, a large farmhouse (B) is indicated. In the middle of the 18th century this became the home of Frances Pawlett. This is the area where Stilton cheese developed in the village of Wymondham in Leicestershire.

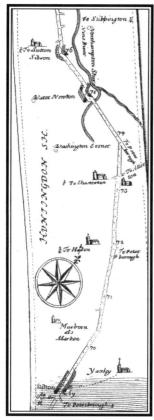

A section from a strip map published in 1675 by John Ogilby as 'cosmographer' to King Charles II. It shows Stilton on the Great North Road.

gallons of milk and five gallons of cream were mixed, then vegetable rennet was added. The curd settled, was cut into lumps and the whey drained off. Salt was then added and the curd was removed, wrapped in linen and then immersed in hot whey for half an hour, before it was removed, wrapped and stacked on wooden shelves. It would then be turned every day for a month, then stored in a cellar to mature and become 'a rich blue cheese'.

The centre for marketing cheese in the town was the Blue Bell Inn, now the Bell Inn. In front of this inn there was a very wide road where daily markets were held. Each year on 16 February the Pedlary Fair was held to start the trading season. Trade was non-stop, with Midlands wool and goods from the Continent arriving via Boston. As this trade decreased the sale of cheese increased, especially Stilton cheese, which was stacked daily in front of the hostelry.

Each May in the early 14th century the Blue Bell Inn was decorated with bluebells to celebrate the arrival of spring. During the winter months, Stilton (Stichiltone) was a bleak fenland town, where the post was delivered on horseback (if it got through at all) and the daily market did not operate. Local traders, dealers, pedlars and hawkers 'wintered down' until the roads became passable again.

On 31 July 1635 Charles I decreed that a continuous series of 'running posts' should be established between London and Edinburgh. One of the staging posts was established at the Bluebell Inn, Stilton, where stables were built to provide a change of horses for travellers or messengers requiring a continuous journey. It was here that the 'post boy', on horseback, was delivering and collecting the mail. The stage coach from Edinburgh to London covered the 400 miles in two days and three nights; it was one of the fastest services on any route. By now the inn at Stilton, still a staging post, was known as the Blue Bell. As a coach arrived at the inn, the coachman sounded his 'post horn', mail was delivered and collected and passengers were warned by the sound of a bell that the coach would soon depart. Eventually the 'blue' was dropped and today this historic pub is called the Bell Inn.

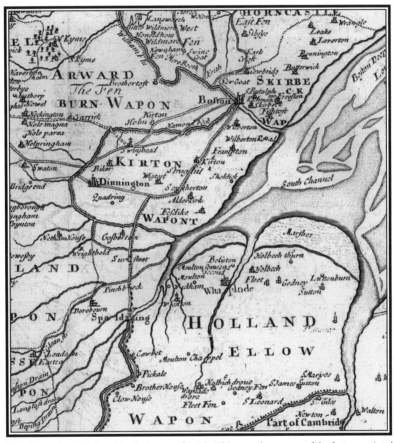

This is a section of Robert Morden's map of 1722. This map shows some of the features printed on Ogilby's strip maps of 1675. Charles II commanded that reliable roads should be maintained to carry horses, carts and carriages; this was essential to ensure that sound roadways existed between important trading centres. The inland port of Boston was connected with the important market at Stilton on Ermine Street. A daily market existed here which traded into London. Goods arrived from all over Europe, but most prominent was corn from the expanding farmland developing in the 'bread basket' of England on the drained fenland. Joseph Thornhill delivered corn to Stilton from Leake, near Boston. He then financed his son, Cooper, who became a leading trader in Stilton during the 18th century.

A 1977 photograph of the mediaeval dairy on the site of the Manor House owned by the lords of the manor of Wymondham, the families of Hamelin (c.1150–1290), Berkeley (1290–1635) and Sedley (1635–c.1700). This building was constructed in three parts: the dairy on the left of the photograph, the maturing room in the centre and the hastener section to the right.

The site of Bevamede Dairies in 1975. In the background is the mediaeval dairy. In the centre left of the photograph are the pig sties and to the right is a new dairy. In this photograph the buildings were used for the production of dried food products. In 2008 this site was cleared and a small housing estate was constructed.

The site of the mediaeval dairy at Wymondham after its conversion into private houses in 2008.

Cooper Thornhill, one of England's greatest horsemen, who once took a bet and rode a famous non-stop ride of 213 miles between London and Stilton in April 1745. Thornhill, along with Mrs Frances Pawlett, who lived in Wymondham from 1742 to 1792, was the East Midlands agent for the London bankers Coutts & Co., buying and selling farm produce. They jointly started the Stilton cheese industry. Large quantities of cheese were sold from the Blue Bell Inn and the Angel Inn, Stilton, by the then owner of these public houses, Cooper Thornhill.

A July 2006 photograph of the Bell Inn, formerly the Blue Bell Inn, Stilton, the birthplace of Stilton cheese. Between the years 1721 and 1730 Richard Bradley, a professor from Cambridge University, published a number of surveys covering agriculture in Huntingdonshire. He stated in 1726 that the landlord of the Blue Bell Inn held a recipe for producing Stilton cheese, which was produced locally as a pressed cream cheese. Cooper Thornhill, with the help of Frances Pawlett, marketed a blue veined unpressed cream cheese from the village of Wymondham which had a more interesting flavour and was made from cows' milk.

The docks at Boston off the Wash in east Lincolnshire, August 2006. This inland port was important for trade into London via the Great North Road and the terminus at the town of Stilton. Trading into this small town began during the 14th century. The volume of traffic resulted in the demand for cheese as an essential easy food, supplied in bulk from the East Midlands. The trade was controlled from the local hostelries. The first record of the Bluebell Inn, Stilton, is dated 1437, when Walter Wyghtfeld was sued for not paying for his wine, which was imported through this port.

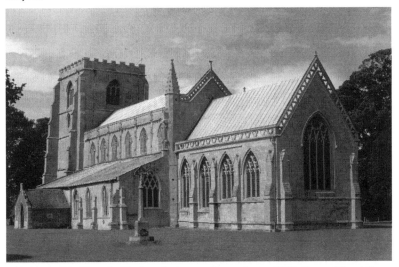

The church of St Mary the Virgin at Leake near Boston, August 2006. Cooper Thornhill was baptised in this church in 1705. He became engaged to Mary in 1730, and in that year he commenced trading out of the small town of Stilton on the Great North Road. He married Mary in the village of Biggleswade, south of Stilton, in 1731.

Receipt to make Stilton Cheese.

TAKE ten Gallons of Morning Milk, and five Gallons of sweet Cream, and beat them together; then put in as much boiling Spring-water, as will make it warmer than Milk from the Cow; when this is done, put in Runnet made strong with large Mace, and when it is come (or the Milk is set in Curd) break it as small as you would do for Cheese-Cakes; and after that salt it, and put it into the Fatt, and press it for two Hours.

Then boil the Whey, and when you have taken off the Curds, put the Cheese into the Whey, and let it stand half an Hour; then put it in the Press, and when you take it out, bind it up for the first Fortnight in Linen Rollers, and turn it upon Boards for the first Month twice a Day.

In 1721 Richard Bradley, a professor of botany at Cambridge University, commenced compiling a treatise on husbandry and gardening. This was published over a 10-year period in monthly parts and hard-bound editions. In it he refers to many types of cheese. In the bound edition of 1726 he refers to a pressed cheese called Stilton cheese. The recipe for this type of cheese was in the possession of the landlord of the Blue Bell Inn, Stilton. This cheese was produced locally, an inferior cheese to the type that was eventually developed by Cooper Thornhill with the help of Frances Pawlett. Cooper needed a fine quality Stilton cheese to sell in London as the Midlands' representative of Coutts & Co., the London bankers.

Many years later when Miss Worthington was running the Angel Inn, now the leading public house in Stilton, she made scathing comments about the cheese produced locally. She displayed an advertisement outside the Angel Inn stating that 'Her cheese was made in Leicestershire, the home of true Stilton Cheese'.

An 18th-century recipe for a pressed cheese produced in farms around Stilton, published in the 1720s by Richard Bradley. It detailed how to prepare a cheese produced in a press, not in a hoop.

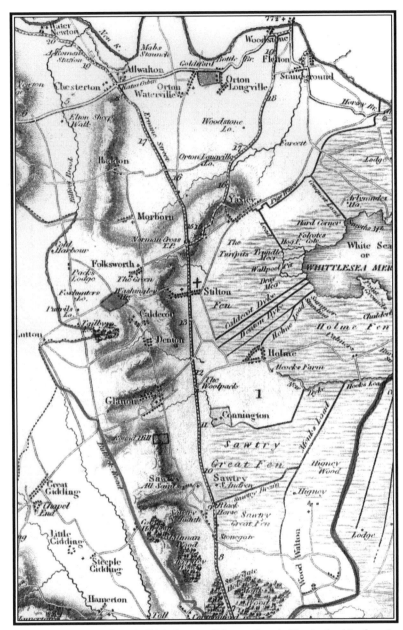

Part of Duncan's map of 1845. This is the area of Norman Cross in Huntingdonshire, featuring Stilton and Stilton Fen. To the west of Ermine Street is the mediaeval sheep-grazing area. Ewes' milk was provided to produce the 'Cheese of Stilton'. To the east is the fenland, which was still in the process of being drained in the middle of the 19th century.

The Bell Inn, Stilton, c.1938. This property was the home and offices of Cooper Thornhill from 1730 to 1759.

The converted farmhouse situated on Edmondthorpe Road, Wymondham, photographed in 2008. It was the home of Frances Pawlett from 1739 to 1797. She developed the modern Stilton cheese in the small dairy situated at the rear of this house in co-operation with Cooper Thornhill.

The Manor House, Wymondham, photographed in 2008. It was constructed by an architect in the Day family living at Wymondham House c.1835 for William Mann, a local farmer who, with the Day family of farmers, made a fortune marketing Stilton cheese to the town of the same name. The same architect designed Stilton House at Stilton. This was eventually demolished because of subsidence caused by its foundations being built in drained fenland.

A cheese fair in the Market Place, Leicester, in 1903. In the foreground stands a collection of 'Leicestershire Wheels', and to the left are some large Stilton cheeses.

The famous Miss Worthington offering a traveller a night's lodging at the Angel Inn, Stilton. This landlady proudly displayed a sign outside her hostelry stating that she sold 'Cheese made in Leicestershire, the home of true Stilton Cheese'. She ran the inn during the early years of the 19th century.

Miss Worthington was the granddaughter of William and Frances Andrews. After William's death, Frances married William Pawlett. It is presumed that Frances Pawlett arranged for the inn to be passed into the hands of her family. The Worthington family lived on Thorne Lane in the village of Wymondham, a short distance from the farmhouse where Frances had lived with her first and second husbands. Worthington House is now situated in the renamed Edmondthorpe Road.

The first 'pony express' was started shortly after 1635. Until reliable carriageways were constructed on the turnpike roads this was the only method of transport for goods and produce other than by horseback or packhorse trains, both of which took much longer. During the summer months wagons drawn by eight horses carried goods along the highways. Charles II commanded that reliable roads should be maintained to carry horses, carts and carriages; this was essential to ensure that sound roadways existed between important trading centres. The inland port of Boston was connected with the important market at Stilton on Ermine Street. A daily market existed here, which traded goods into London. Produce arrived from all over Europe and cereals were sold in large

An engraving from a letterhead, which was used in the early part of the 19th century. During the golden age for the marketing of Stilton cheese in the town of Stilton (from the 1780s to the 1840s) possibly involved with the Bell Hotel on Humberstone Gate, Leicester and the Blue Bell Inn, Stilton. Many contractors supplied this small town on the Great North Road with blue veined Stilton cheese.

Elizabeth Spooner was such an entrepreneur, and she factored Stilton cheese in and around Leicester and conveyed it to Stilton and other outlets on a regular basis, using a lightly constructed four-wheeled postillion-driven chaise. This was a very fast carriage, with a movable hood. The horses were controlled by the driver riding on the back of the nearside horse.

amounts, brought over from the newly-drained fens. Joseph Thornhill was one of those who delivered corn to Stilton from Leake, near Boston. He then financed his son, Cooper, who became a leading trader at Stilton in the 18th century.

Cooper Thornhill was one of England's greatest horsemen, who lived between the years of 1705 and 1759. He was born in the village of Leake, north-east of Boston in Lincolnshire. Cooper often visited Stilton with his father, Joseph, who traded in corn, and he later took up a position as an underwriter with the London banker Coutts & Co., trading out of Cornhill, London. He soon found that he needed a Midlands office, and, as Stilton is on Ermine Street only 70 miles north of London, he chose that town to be his Midlands base. He married his wife, Mary, in the parish church at Biggleswade in 1731, when he was 25 and that year he purchased the Blue Bell Inn at Stilton. He expanded his business into farming produce, with wool being the most prominent source of income.

The market held on the wide main street in the centre of Stilton was supported by pedlars, hawkers and various traders. The buying and consumption of a wide variety of cheeses played an important part in the economy of this small trading town. The fens were being drained and that meant that wheat, oats and barley became important commodities (especially barley for the production of beer) along with fine cheese, all of which found a ready market in London. A soft blue-veined cheese had become very popular in the capital, which was produced locally in small amounts, while large quantities were delivered from the village of Wymondham, Leicestershire. However, there was insufficient Stilton cheese produced locally to cater for demand and Cooper saw an opportunity to increase his business. As a horseman, he had visited many farmers trading in these products, including Frances and William Pawlett, who lived in Wymondham.

An Edwardian Stilton scoop. These special spoons were introduced in the late 18th century for large family gatherings in the villages around Melton Mowbray. Stilton was, and still is, served with a spoon on some tables after the sweet course has been eaten. The traditional ritual is that the host introduces the port to the left of the table and the Stilton to the right, which is served with a Stilton scoop to extract the cheese from a half Stilton.

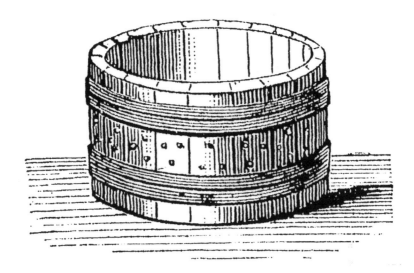

An engraving of an 18th-century bottomless wooden cheese mould/hoop used in the production of the early type of Stilton cheese.

The cheese-producing village of Wymondham was ideally placed for his needs and he entered into a trading agreement with the couple.

Frances Pawlett was a splendid cheese-maker and by 1743 Cooper and Frances were controlling most of the Stilton cheese produced in the East Midlands. In 1730 Cooper purchased the Angel Inn that was opposite the Blue Bell Inn and constructed a series of vaults under the inn for storing and maturing Stilton cheese. This new location enabled him to factor cheese to London, greatly improving his business. The Pawletts then began instructing Leicestershire and Rutland farmers on the 'modern' method of producing Stilton cheese in their dairies. One Leicestershire entrepreneur who took their advice on board was Shuckburgh Ashby of Quenby Hall, who entered into a contract to supply cheese to the Bell Inn in 1759, the year Cooper Thornhill died. After his death the landlord was a local businessman, A.B. Clark.

With the improvement of the highway by the turnpike trusts, travel increased along Ermine Street, now the Great North Road. Most travellers going north stopped at the small market town of Stilton, and between 1780 and 1790 the competition to provide refreshments for the coach trade was intense. At the Blue Bell Inn the speciality on offer was Stilton cheese. From the 1780s until the late 1840s coaches stopped both day and night, and the inn offered a continuous service. The volume of traffic was enormous: approximately 300 horses were stabled at the Blue Bell Inn and an equal number at the Angel Inn and at other hostelries. Horses were grazed on the high ground to the west.

The sheep trade had disappeared and no cheese was made in the locality; from the 1780s it was imported from Leicestershire and Rutland. Miss Worthington, the granddaughter of Frances Pawlett, ran the Angel Inn in the early years of the 19th century, possibly bought by Frances from Orme Bailey (Thornhill's second wife) after Thornhill's death.

Four members of staff filling the boot of a coach in the yard of the Blue Bell Inn, Stilton, c.1840. Among the packages lies a brace of mallard obtained from Stilton Fen and a well-wrapped Stilton cheese.

Cornhill, London c.1900. Site of the Exchange for corn and cheese and Cooper Thornhill's offices in the early part of the 18th century.

The Corn Exchange, leading into Lombard Street, Cornhill, London, 1750.

An engraving of the new Corn Exchange in London, which was erected in 1828.

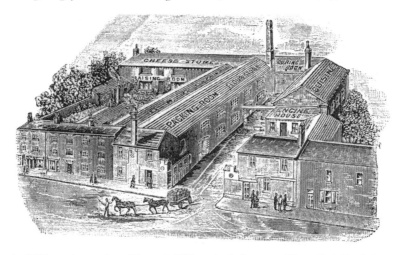

An 1892 wood engraving of Evans & Hill's pork pie factory on Thorpe End. Enoch Evans opened a grocer's shop in Queen's Street in 1830 before moving to the Beast Market in 1840, where he began making pork pies. In 1859 he started building the factory illustrated above. Opened in 1860, this was the first purpose-built factory to produce Melton Mowbray pork pies commercially. To the rear of this factory is the maturing room for Stilton cheese, which was also factored through the factory by Evans. In 1910 Henry Morris purchased this factory. He raised pigs to consume the surplus whey, a by-product of cheese production. He then converted the pork into pies!

The golden years of stage-coach travel were from the 1790s to the 1840s, and during this period the marketing of Stilton cheese from the town peaked. There must have been hundreds of suppliers, controlled by many middle men, and legends were established and fortunes made by the lucky Leicestershire farmers, especially in the village of Wymondham, a parish very close to the vital trade route of the Great North Road.

The opening of the Midland and the Great Northern railway lines connecting Peterborough with London in the early 1840s heralded the beginning of the end of the stage-coach business, and the golden years of the Stilton cheese trade also came to an end. The coaching trade continued locally, but the long-distance coach

---

The Sudbury Dairy Co., Ltd.,
SUDBURY, Nʀ. DERBY.

DEPARTMENTS—

BUTTER.	**BUTTERMILK.**
CREAM.	**STILTON CHEESE.**
WHOLE MILK.	**DERBYSHIRE CHEESE.**
SEPARATED MILK.	**FANCY CHEESE.**
CREAM CHEESE.	

Contracts entered into with Hospitals, Institutions, and other large Consumers.

London Depots—

172, Wardour Street, Oxford Street, W.
138, Vernon Chambers, Theobald's Road, W.C.
18, Sandringham Buildings, Charing Cross Road, W.C.
107, Goswell Road, Aldersgate Street, E.C.
27, Bell Street, Edgware Road, W.   79, Mortimer Street, W.
12A, New Street, Covent Garden, W.C.   15, Crowndale Road, N.W.
155, Old Street, E.C.   9, Cromer Street, Gray's Inn Road.

Postal and Telegraphic Address : "BATES, SUDBURY, DERBY."
London   ,,   ,,   "MODERATE, LONDON."
Railway Address : "SUDBURY," North Stafford Railway and
              Great Northern Railway.   [15]

An advertisement for a very large dairy in Derbyshire from 1891. This dairy produced a variety of cheeses, including Stilton cheese, which were marketed throughout London. In 1904 the New Sudbury dairy had been formed and the manager was Tom Bates.

trade ceased, as did the wholesale marketing of cheese from Stilton. As a result the historic local market collapsed. The Leicestershire farmers marketed their product through wholesalers via the railway system direct to London. Gradually, because of loss of trade, the fine coaching inns around Stilton fell into disrepair and many of them closed down. In 1894, parish councils were created. It was decided that Stilton no longer warranted its label as a market town and it was downgraded to the status of a village.

In 1847 large quantities of Stilton cheese were delivered to London from Melton Mowbray railway station. By then the majority of Stilton cheese was made in and around that town. In September 1883 the first Stilton Cheese Fair was held on the site of the Market Cross close to the railway station. From this date onwards Melton Mowbray became the centre for Stilton cheese production, taking over from Stilton, the small, forgotten market town on Ermine Street.

At the height of the Stilton cheese trade in the early part of the 19th century, there was hardly a farm grazing cows for milk production in east Leicestershire, the Lincolnshire wolds, the Vale of Belvoir and parts of Rutland that did not convert its surplus milk to Stilton cheese. Like so many other products that have a long history, legends develop and are combined with tradition. In legend the premier village of Stilton cheese making is considered to be Wymondham, which does admittedly have a long history of cheese production. As a result of the 16th-century enclosures, many farmers manufactured unpressed cheese, and the probate inventories covering farmers who died with cheese stored in their cheese chambers and dairies are too numerous to list. Two farmers were particularly important: William Whitworth, who died in 1618, and Richard Berriffe, who died in 1686 with his probate inventory proved on 6 March. They were both making an unpressed cream cheese that would have been equivalent to a Stilton cheese. In Berriffe's cheese chamber he had two hasteners, 18 cheeses, one salt barrel, three cheese boards and two curd vessels. In his dairy were four pails, one churn, six panchions, nine shelves, one pair of weights and spring, three cheese vats (troughs) and two cheese boards. Some of his farmland used for grazing was on Crabtree Wong, near the Stapleford/Wymondham border. The legendary Mrs Pawlett made cheese at Wymondham and it is because of her association with Cooper Thornhill that Stilton cheese gained its place in the history of England.

Many historians have credited Mrs Frances Pawlett as being the inventor of Stilton cheese, a myth that has been perpetuated for more than 200 years since

William Marshall's two-volume *Rural economy of the Midlands Counties* was published in 1790. Mrs Pawlett (née Pick) was certainly involved in the manufacture of Stilton cheese at an early age, and it is likely that she standardized the blue-veined cheese that bears the name, but credit for inventing the cheese cannot be given entirely to her. The first recorded reference to a cheese called Stilton was made in 1722, when Frances Pawlett would have been two years of age. From the reference, we know that a cheese called Stilton existed long before she began her career as a supreme dairywoman and cheese-maker. A commercially produced blue-veined cream cheese had certainly been marketed from this parish by generations of farmers' wives, and we must therefore credit them with Stilton's invention even if they did not attach the name.

Frances Pawlett was born at Sproxton, Leicestershire, in 1720, the second daughter of Richard and Dorothy Pick. Frances married twice. Her first husband was William Andrews, whom she married at Buckminster on 31 January 1739. They had one child, Richard. Andrews died in 1741 and on 13 October 1742 Frances married William Pawlett, a bachelor of Market Overton, Rutland, in South Witham church, Lincolnshire. They had no children. William was the son of William Pawlett of Market Overton and Mary Adcock of Hambleton, Rutland, and was born in 1712. Frances set up home in a farmhouse on Edmondthorpe Road with William Andrews and then William Pawlett. They rented the house and nearby farmland.

Frances was taught the art of cheese-making by her mother. She is believed to have standardized the shape and weight of the cheese, developed the procedure of hand crumbling and packing the curd into a ceramic mould similar to an earthenware drainpipe, with holes pierced throughout the sides of a bottomless container, in order to develop a firm crust. The blue mould formed more quickly when the maturing cheeses were pierced with large needles to speed up the process, and Frances is said to have developed this technique. She is also credited with calling the blue-veined cream cheese, which had been made by various recipes and a variety of people in Wymondham for many centuries, her Stilton cheese, made to her recipe!

The Pawletts were Rutland farmers, shrewd in business. William was aware of Frances's skill as a Stilton cheese-maker and saw the marriage as an ideal partnership for the producing and marketing of large quantities of cheese. As a farmer, William Pawlett had contact with Cooper Thornhill in his capacity as a

The gravestone in Wymondham churchyard of William Pawlett (1712–87) and Frances Pawlett (1718–1808). Frances developed a cheese that had been made in Wymondham for many centuries. With Cooper Thornhill she perfected a formula that was different from the one used by Thornhill's predecessor at the Blue Bell Inn at Stilton. Her recipe produced a quality cheese, not the inferior variety that was being made in some dairies.

Richard Adkinson's advertisement of 1898. He was the leading factor of cheeses out of Leicester. This company traded from the end of the 19th century until the 1940s, and their speciality was Leicestershire and Stilton cheese. He did not trade in Leicester cheese as he considered this to be an inferior product.

corn buyer. Both Pawlett and Thornhill were aware of the potential of cheese sales into London, so they entered into a trading agreement. The Great North Road ran only a few miles to the east of Wymondham and Market Overton, and Frances and her husband William utilized it in their successful business partnership with Cooper Thornhill. In 1743 they were selling him large quantities of cheese for retail at the Bell and Angel inns at Stilton until William died in 1787. Frances had been factoring Stilton cheese for more than 40 years and this had made her a very wealthy woman, so she retired and went to live at Little Dalby. She later wrote her own will, in which her skill as a shrewd businesswoman was very apparent. Frances died on Christmas Eve 1808 and was buried beside her husband William on 28 December in the churchyard at Wymondham.

In the 21st century the Vale of Belvoir is considered to be the historic centre of Stilton cheese production. Unfortunately, research cannot support this observation, as the enclosure awards had still not been completed in the Vale by 1794. Before then little or no drainage existed and the open field system of winter marshland was not suitable for supporting large herds of cows throughout the year. Stilton cheese was being produced in small quantities by local farmers raising cows on fine pasture land at Little Dalby, Laund, Withcote, Quenby, Kirby Bellars and Wymondham. The farmers in Leighfield Forest on the Rutland and

In 1875 Thomas Nuttall altered his Leicester cheese dairy at the Manor House, Beeby, to produce Stilton cheese on factory lines, employing 30 people. On his expanding dairy farm he needed to house more farm workers, so he built a row of farm workers cottages at Little Beeby in 1876. This is the end wall of these cottages, photographed in April 2008.

Thomas Nuttall and Charlotte Fairbrother, Stilton cheese-makers from Beeby, at the cheese fair in Leicester, 1903. (Reproduced by kind permission of Leicestershire Museums, Arts and Records Service.)

An illustration of a Victorian cheese vat; the curd is being cut.

The cheese factory buildings developed by Thomas Nuttall at the Manor House, Beeby, near Leicester, in 1875. The property is now converted into private houses, photographed in May 1994.

HARRY SCAMPTON,

(LATE W. SCAMPTON,)

Stilton Cheese Factor

AND

PROVISION MERCHANT,

5 & 7, NEW BOND STREET,

LEICESTER.

Harry Scampton, a Stilton cheese factor in Leicester in 1880.

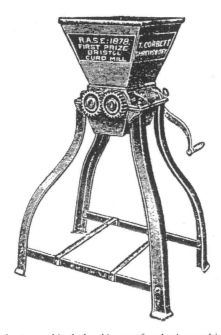

A curd cutter used in the breaking up of curd prior to salting, 1878.

An engraving of Belvoir Castle, 1800. Below Blackberry Hill is Belvoir Castle Dairy. In this dairy a Mrs Stilton was producing Stilton cheese from cows grazing on pastures in the Vale of Belvoir.

Dairy Crest Dairy, London Lane, Wymeswold, c.1985. This building was originally constructed as a primitive Methodist chapel and has since been demolished to make way for an old peoples' home. The village of Wymeswold has a long tradition of Stilton cheese production. In the early part of the 20th century it supported six Stilton cheese dairies, the earliest of which was the cheese-making dairy of Samuel Daft, who was well established by 1899, making Stilton on Church Street. The building shown in this photograph was converted into a dairy by Emberlin & Co. Ltd, and was later purchased by J.M. Nuttall's of Hartington in Derbyshire. This was the largest dairy, though it still only produced approximately 50 Stiltons per day.

A Stilton cheese hoop made by Alfred Ladbury & Son, 3 High Street, Melton Mowbray. Used by Mrs Doris Wright of Ingersby Lodge Farm from 1920 until 1961.

Leicestershire border produced a large amount of Stilton cheese that was exported to the town of Stilton.

A number of families became involved throughout East Leicestershire, and the village of Harby became a centre for Stilton cheese production in the Vale of Belvoir. The female members of the Starbuck family were responsible for converting a row of three cottages into a dairy, hastener and maturing room, and it is believed that their cheese was factored by William Thorpe Tuxford, who

A prime Stilton cheese.

traded in the 1830s. George Baguley, a farmer in this village, produced his own cheese and factored it to London and Leicester.

The leading entrepreneur of pressed and Stilton cheese was Thomas Nuttall (1835–1926). In the 1860s he was factoring cheese out of Derbyshire and Leicestershire. Nuttall had been producing Stilton cheese in his dairy at Uttoxeter by 1880 and in 1883 at Etwall. Without doubt Thomas Nuttall became the leading Stilton cheese manufacturer in the world: his produce won first prizes in the Midlands, London, Amsterdam and New York. It was through his marketing techniques that Stilton cheese became the 'King of English Cheeses'.

In 1880 Henry Morris began producing Stilton cheese from the Manor House Farm at Saxelbye, and a few years later he converted a row of cottages on the main street in this village to produce cheese. Today this is still one of the smallest dairies producing Stilton cheese. Henry Morris formed a co-operative with various cheese-makers at Stathern, Eastwell, Wymeswold and his own farm at Saxelbye. He purchased Thomas Nuttall's dairy on North Street, Melton Mowbray, in 1900 and Wymondham Dairy from the Day family at about the same time. In 1910 he purchased Evans & Hill's pork pie factory on Thorpe End, Melton Mowbray and expanded into pie production, using the existing cheese maturing room for factoring Stilton cheese. He died in 1920 and his cheese empire was broken up.

In 1860 Horatio Emberlin was factoring Stilton cheese from the Exchange in Market Place, Leicester, and selling this cheese in his grocers shop on 18 Gallowtree Gate. He had begun by factoring many local cheeses, including Leicester and Leicestershire, but because Stilton's popularity and price soared Emberlin and his family decided not only to factor Stilton cheese, but also to manufacture the product. The leading village for Stilton production in the late 19th and the early 20th century was Harby in the Vale of Belvoir, and Emberlin decided to set up his dairy there to be part of the competition. Emberlin and Co. Ltd started business as Stilton cheese-makers in 1911 in Harby, operating as Belvoir Vale Dairies. They were eventually bought out by Wiltshire United Dairies in 1920. In 1912 they had purchased the primitive Methodist chapel on London Road in Wymeswold and converted it into a small Stilton cheese dairy. This property was then sold to Joe Brindley in 1948, who also owned Nuttall's dairy in Hartington, Derbyshire, and it was eventually owned by Davy Crest.

A cheese fair in the Market Square, Melton Mowbray, c.1900. These fairs were held three times a year, the last one being held on 18 November 1915. In the centre of this photograph stand Mr and Mrs Gilbert of Great Dalby, who were among the organisers of the fairs. Mrs Mary Musson, wearing a straw hat, is standing on the right.

Companies factoring cheese as middlemen controlled the price of cheese, and this annoyed many farmers. Between them Nuttall, Morris and Emberlin were controlling the sale of Stilton cheese, particularly to the farmers producing milk in the Vale of Belvoir.

In the 1890s, Joseph Stevenson, a farmer and grazier, was running a tenanted farm on land owned by the Duke of Rutland in Hose, with his son Thomas Hoe Stevenson. He expanded part of his herd of cows to produce more milk in 1894. Five years later, in 1899, Thomas Hoe was running his father's farm in Hose and wished to expand into dairy farming. By 1902 he was running a large farm in fields near Long Clawson on the Rutland Estates. His milk was purchased by Henry Morris, who dominated the Stilton cheese trade in the Vale of Belvoir, controlling the wholesale price of milk. On 6 November 1911 Thomas Hoe Stevenson formed a co-operative with 11 other farmers to produce Stilton cheese in their own dairy, the Long Clawson Dairy. Thomas Hoe was the first chairman. Born in 1848, he was influenced by his father and developed an interest in soft cheese production. He died in 1937.

The new co-operative purchased the Royal Oak public house and on this site the dairy was built. They employed the skilled cheese-maker Tom Stockdale, who was followed by William McNair. The continued success of this dairy lies in the fact that it is still a farmers' co-operative, obtaining top-quality milk from its members. Consolidated in the 1930s, it was one of the leading forces behind the formation of the Stilton Cheese Makers' Association.

In the village of Colston Bassett in 1912 16 farmers formed a co-operative similar to the one formed in Long Clawson. These farmers had a share capital of £16. From a deposit of only £256 an excellent Stilton cheese dairy materialised. Eliza Wagstaff, a fine local cheese-maker, was appointed manager. Today five farmers support this dairy and provide excellent milk from their cows grazing in the Vale of Belvoir.

A hastener used by Frank Fryer in his Stilton cheese dairy at Grange Farm, Somerby, Leicestershire, in 1935. The cheese hoops containing the crumbled curd were stacked on the shelves to drain off the whey, which was caught in a bowl under the centre of the bottom shelf. This hastener is now on display in the Carnegie Museum at Melton Mowbray.

This is a fine descriptive drawing of one of Henry Morris's farmhouse dairies in 1919.

An 1897 photograph of Mary Elizabeth Brothwell, who became manageress of Henry Morris's Wymondham Dairy, on the junction of Main Street and Edmondthorpe Road. She married William Ward and died in October 1961 aged 79. Mary was buried in Wymondham churchyard, alongside many other fine Stilton cheese-makers.

A Stilton cheese fair in the marketplace at Melton Mowbray, c.1900. In the centre of the background is F. Warner's shop, which manufactured Melton Mowbray pork pies.

Wymondham Dairy when it was owned by Henry Morris, c.1910. The photograph shows Stilton cheese-producing equipment which has been positioned outside the dairy to drain. Left to right: Mrs Bratby, Miss Briggs, Mrs W. Harris and Miss S. Chafer (manageress). These four cheese-makers are displaying examples of their cheese.

Wymondham Dairy, 1996. Bevamede Dairies built this factory style extension onto the front of the Old Manor House in the 1930s. It closed in 1940. Stilton cheese ceased to be produced, and the building was sold to William Hill. In 2008 this building was demolished and houses erected on the site.

In 1835 William Thorpe Tuxford was factoring Stilton cheese from the Market Place in Melton Mowbray. It is presumed that he took over this business from his father who, it is believed, was factoring cheese in the 1780s from farmers producing cheese around Melton Mowbray.

In 1867 Messrs Tebbutt and Crosher, gentlemen's outfitters, decided to change their method of making a living by moving into the expanding pork pie business. Taking into the partnership William Thorpe Tuxford of Tuxford & Nephews, Stilton cheese factors, the two firms combined and shared the same premises on Thorpe End, Melton Mowbray. The pies were marketed under the name Tebbutt & Co., while the cheese was marketed under the name Tuxford & Nephews. John Francis Crosher started making Stilton cheese in Tuxford & Nephews' warehouse at Thorpe End, Melton Mowbray, in 1909. From 1928 both manufacturing processes were marketed under one company name, Tuxford and Tebbutt Ltd. In 1966 they closed down the pork pie side of their business and concentrated on the production of Stilton and Red Leicester cheese.

Through the formation of the Stilton Cheese Makers' Association in 1936 it was no longer possible to produce Stilton cheese in any county other than Derbyshire, Nottinghamshire and Leicestershire. Fine cheeses were made in other counties, especially Somerset. In 1947 Frank Strickland-Skailes expanded his

Somerset cheese-making enterprises into Leicestershire, as he already owned the Cropwell Bishop Creamery. He purchased the dairy in North Street, Melton Mowbray, and obtained a 50 per cent holding in Waltham Dairy. Milk for both these dairies was pasteurised at Cropwell Bishop. In the early 1970s the operations in Somerset ceased, and all cheese production became concentrated at Melton Mowbray and Cropwell Bishop. Strickland-Skailes was producing Melton Mowbray Farmers' Coloured Cheddar, Devon Squire Cheddar, Melton Mowbray Dairy Farmers' Caerphilly, Golden Counties Melton Mowbray Stilton and Red Leicester at the Melton Mowbray dairy on North Street in 1986. All the cheese is now produced at Cropwell Bishop Creamery in Nottinghamshire.

The dairy on North Street, Melton Mowbray was built by Thomas Nuttall in the 1880s, and was sold to Henry Morris in about 1900. After Henry Morris's death in 1920, it was purchased by the Melton Dairy Farmers. In 1948 it came into the ownership of the Skailes family and was run by Cropwell Bishop Creamery until 1986, when the Stilton cheese production was transferred to Cropwell Bishop. During the interwar years Mabel Tyers was the dairy manageress, and she had also worked at the John O'Gaunt dairy. It is not possible to list all of the Stilton cheese-makers who were producing this cheese in small dairies and as seasonal cheese on very many farms in the East Midlands.

The main method of marketing Stilton cheese out of east Leicestershire was through factoring. Very many of the farmhouse dairies produced only a few cheeses each week, to be purchased and sold by middlemen. In the 1830s William Mann, the Day family and relatives of Frances Pawlett had almost a complete monopoly supplying the town of Stilton with cheese, while Melton Mowbray was developing as a centre for factoring Stilton. There were five warehouses factoring Stilton cheese to the extensive cheese markets at Leicester from Melton Mowbray. These warehouses included those owned by Thomas Baker, Market Place; Robert Judd, High Street; Thomas Mayfield, Market Place; William Thorpe Tuxford, Market Place and David Wall, Market Place.

In the 1860s Horatio Edwin Emberlin began factoring cheese into Leicester from Melton Mowbray and selling it in the Market Place. Nephews of Tuxford were operating from a warehouse on Sherrard Street in Melton Mowbray. There were a number of small outlets in the county factoring Stilton cheese, and one was owned by John Dickenson, who later became the leading Melton Mowbray pork pie manufacturer.

A 1938 advertisement for Bevamede Dairies, whose offices were situated at the rear of Wicklow Lodge, off Burton Road. The warehouse was in Park Lane off Leicester Street, Melton Mowbray. The main Stilton-producing dairy was at Wymondham, with two supporting dairies at Hickling Pastures and Nether Broughton.

Mabel Tyers, manageress at the North Street dairy in Melton Mowbray, testing her Stiltons in 1970. Before working for Somerset Creameries Mabel ran the Stilton cheese-producing dairy at John O'Gaunt.

Peter Allcock cutting the curd at Hartington dairy, 1978.

Colin Dunn spreading salt over the curd in the Hartington Stilton cheese dairy, 1988.

The Stilton cheese-producing dairy at Twyford, c.1925, which later became part of John O'Gaunt dairy. It was demolished in 1943 after a lorry belonging to the American army crashed into it!

Margaret Partridge and Elaine Miltner are smoothing the surface of young Stiltons with flat knives in the dairy at Hartington, 1978. In the background the salted, crumbled curd is settling into plastic cheese moulds/hoops.

Alan Salt, Stilton cheese-maker, and Trevor Hickman, at the Hartington Dairy shop, spring 2001. Alan is promoting Stilton cheese and Trevor is promoting his book.

The Stilton cheese-making dairy at Harby in 2001. In 1988 Millway Foods was formed following a management buyout of the St Ivel Unigate Dairy at Harby. In 1990 the company was bought by Bongrain, a French-based international food company specialising in dairy products. This company sold the cheese-making dairy to Dairy Crest Ltd in 1999, who closed the factory in the spring of 2001 and transferred the production of cheese to Hartington.

Jean Morris cutting the curd at Long Clawson dairy in 1975. This task is undertaken one and a half hours after the rennet has been added and the curd has solidified. Cutting the curd releases the whey.

Curd milling at Long Clawson Dairy, 1975. This process breaks up the curd into walnut-sized pieces. Henrietta Widdowson is bending down into the machine to check the quality.

Neil Bailey and Peter Tinsley displaying prize-winning Stilton cheese produced by Long Clawson Dairy in December 2000.

Karlis Doughty testing Stilton cheese in the extensive maturing warehouse at Long Clawson Dairy in 1999.

Edith Stevens ladling curd into cooler trays at Colston Bassett Dairy, 1975.

Colston Bassett Dairy, July 2006. Dawn Wilks is rubbing Stilton cheese to form the crust; in the background a mould (hoop) is being removed from a formed cheese by Norma Wilks.

A cutter used for cutting curd to release the whey.

James Stokes, Chairman of Colston Bassett and District Dairy Ltd, selling his company's Stilton cheese at the Melton Mowbray farmers' market in May 2000.

Billy Kevan with the prize-winning Stilton cheese produced at Colston Bassett Dairy. It won first prize, the famous Easom Bowl, at the Melton Mowbray Fatstock Society Show in November 2008.

Bill Grennells sorting boxes of cheeses for distribution from the packing department at Cropwell Bishop in 1971, including Melton Mowbray Farmers' Coloured Cheddar, Devon Squire Cheddar, Melton Mowbray Dairy Farmers' Caerphilly and Golden Counties Melton Mowbray Stilton. This dairy obtained a fine reputation for producing excellent Red Leicester cheese in their dairy at Cropwell Bishop.

The 'Old Dairy', North Street, Melton Mowbray. Built for Thomas Nuttall in the 1880s, it was sold to Henry Morris in 1900. After Henry Morris's death in 1920, it was purchased by the Melton Dairy Farmers. In 1936 it came into the ownership of Matthew Skailes and was run by Cropwell Bishop Creamery until 1986, when the Stilton cheese production was transferred to Cropwell Bishop. During the interwar years Mabs Tyers was the dairy manageress, and under her leadership the dairy produced excellent Stilton cheese.

At the 1997 Melton Mowbray Fatstock Society Show the coveted Easom Bowl for the best Stilton cheese was awarded to Cropwell Bishop Creamery. Left to right: Mario Addesso, cheese-maker; Ian Skailes, director; Linda Cregan, packaging manager; Andy Robinson, operations manager; and Howard Lucas, Stilton production manager.

Tuxford & Tebbutt dairy on Thorpe End, Melton Mowbray, April 2008. Producers of fine Stilton cheese and occasionally Leicester cheese.

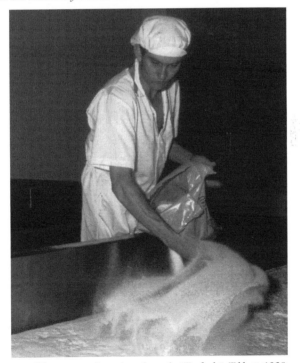

Peter Wharton spreading salt on the curd at Tuxford & Tebbutt, 1990.

The Stilton cheese production line at Tuxford & Tebbutt in 1990. The vats, draining table and the conveyor to the crumbling system are all visible.

Wendy Berners and Trish Hughes in Tuxford and Tebbutt's dairy, rubbing up Stilton cheese to form the crust, 1988.

Sara Strong adding the starter into the cheese vat containing pasteurised milk in the new dairy at Quenby Hall, 2005.

John Lambert and Sara Strong with a cheese hoop and a Quenby Stilton at the entrance to the original dairy at Quenby Hall in 2005.

Mark Frapwell at Webster's Dairy in 1999. Mark is displaying the dairy's organic Blue Stilton cheese.

Webster's Dairy at Saxelbye as it looked in 1920, when it was owned by Henry Morris. In the photograph curd is draining in the leads. When the whey had drained away, the curd was broken up, salted and packed into the hoops stacked in the background. Leads are no longer used in the modern industry.

Quenby Hall, c.1920. The Quenby estate has been a notable area for cheese production in Leicestershire since the Saxon period. It became a centre for Stilton cheese production after 1759, principally marketing this cheese in the famous Leicester and London markets. c760: Quenby began life as Cwene-burg, an Anglo-Saxon queen's manor. Her name was Cynethuyth and she was the wife of the Saxon King Offa. At that time the settlement comprised a group of houses in the open countryside of Leicestershire. The ewe's milk from the village's flocks was made into an unpressed cream cheese during the summer months. 1066: By this time Quenby was an Anglo-Saxon hamlet in the rolling open fields, with vast flocks of sheep owned by the inhabitants. The surrounding pastures came under the control of King William I and his conquering generals, who generated revenue from wool, cheese and mutton. 1377: The hamlet of Quenby contained 10 houses whose inhabitants lived off the land, raised sheep and produced seasonal unpressed cream cheese. 1485: The Ashby family began enclosing the open fields to lay out the park and farmland, which destroyed the small hamlet at Quenby. 1489: The Ashbys were raising speciality sheep and some cattle, and they produced a seasonal cheese in their farmhouse dairy and in outlying farmhouses. 1615: George Ashby began building the present Jacobean house on the site of a farmhouse next to the purpose-built dairy, which made cheese from cows' and ewes' milk. 1620: The Ashbys marketed sheep, cattle and cheese. 1664: John Ornby marketed pressed Leicestershire cheese from the Quenby estate to Cornhill in London. c.1670: Lady Mary Beaumont, daughter of Sir Erasmus de la Fontaine of Kirby Bellars, gave her improved recipe for making a pressed cheese to the Ashbys of Quenby Hall. c.1700: Elizabeth Scarborough ran the dairy at Quenby Hall and was producing a lightly pressed Quenby cheese, coloured orange, which was set in the shape of a child's drum. 1715: Because of financial difficulties, the dairy and hall were vacated by the Ashby family and their farming business was controlled from one of their other estates. The Quenby pressed cheese was then produced by Elizabeth Orton, née Scarborough, at Little Dalby, although the Ashby name was retained. 1759: Warring Ashby sold the Quenby farming estate to Shuckburgh Ashby, an entrepreneur dealing in cheese, to raise large herds of cattle to produce cheese to be sold in Leicester and the London markets. Cooper Thornhill, William and Frances Pawlett and Shuckburgh Ashby entered into an arrangement to market Stilton cheese from the farmhouse dairy at Quenby Hall. Shuckburgh Ashby met Cooper Thornhill at his offices in Cornhill, London, when both of them were dealing in cheese; Thornhill with Stilton cheese, Ashby with pressed Leicestershire cheese. They were both aware that for the London market the manufacture and promotion of unpressed cheese produced a much more reliable source of income than pressed cheese. 1759: After the death of Cooper Thornhill at Stilton, the Pawletts of Wymondham and Ashbys of Quenby were producing a considerable amount of the Stilton cheese made in Leicestershire and Rutland and sold at Stilton, Huntingdonshire. 1787: When William Pawlett died, Frances Pawlett negotiated the sale of Quenby Stilton cheese and cheese from other farms, until her retirement in 1803. 1792: Shuckburgh Ashby died. The production of Stilton at Quenby dairy entered into a slow decline. c.1880 Farms on the Quenby estate were only producing small amounts of blue-veined cream cheese for local consumption, and eventually production of this farmhouse cream cheese at Quenby ceased. In November 2005 world-famous Stilton cheese was produced once again in the dairy at Quenby Hall.

A 1929 photograph of Larkbarrow Farm on Exmoor, Somerset. In 1850 Stilton cheese was produced in the dairy at this farm and sold direct to the London markets. During World War Two this farmhouse was used for artillery target practice and demolished.

At about this time there were attempts to produce and factor cheese in other counties out of the East Midlands, with little or no results. The exception was on Exmoor in Somerset. The Knight family opened up the countryside near Porlock and paid for the construction of a railway. They constructed two farmhouse complexes. The main one was Larkbarrow Farm, built in the 1840s. In 1850 they let the tenancy to James Meadows from Leicestershire, and he set up a dairy, using the milk that he obtained from the cows that were grazing on the fine pastures. He produced excellent Stilton cheese, which he marketed into London by train. Unfortunately, parts of Exmoor were developed into a deer hunting reserve and by 1900 Larkbarrow farmhouse had become a 'hunting and shooting box'.

At the turn of the 20th century there was a leap forward in the production and marketing of Stilton cheese. In a survey published in 1904 the following dairies were recorded as making Stilton cheese, with many of them also recorded as being involved in the marketing of their produce. The leading producer in Leicestershire was Henry Morris, who was operating out of Saxelbye, North Street Melton Mowbray, Stathern and Wymondham, and he purchased four further dairies. Smaller producers included: Samuel Daft, Church Street, Wymeswold; Furmidge & Kemp, Harby; William Green, Harby; John James, Brook Street, Wymeswold; operating moderately were Miss E. Lamin, Scalford; Mrs Bethsheba Marriott, Nether Broughton; The Scalford Dairy, Miss Margaret Rouse, Scalford; Mary Jane Starbuck, Harby; Ybele Gerard Veen, Harby. In Nottinghamshire: John Clements, Plungar; Miss A. Miller, Plungar; William Miller, Plungar. In Derbyshire: John Marriott Nuttall, Hartington; William Nuttall, Ashbourne, Sutton Cheese Factory (H. Bridges owner), Sutton-on-the-Hill, Derby. According to the published records all of the cheese factors in this part of the Midlands dealt in a wide range of cheese.

When World War One broke out in 1914 there were 13 speciality Stilton cheese dairies operating on factory lines, three of which were in Nottinghamshire and two in Derbyshire. Many farmers in villages around Melton Mowbray produced Stilton cheese during the summer months, and this was sold privately or factored by dealers. However, many dairies closed during World War One. During World War Two all Stilton cheese dairies were closed. Some of the commercial dairies survived, and one or two farmers tried to produce Stilton cheese, but they could not match the price of the large commercial dairies. The last commercially-run farmhouse dairy in the area closed in 1961; this was the extensive farmhouse dairy at Model Farm, Ingarsby Lodge, near Beeby, which was controlled by Mrs Doris Marion Wright.

In 1940 there were 17 dairies producing Stilton cheese in Leicestershire, and in that year they were all instructed not to produce Stilton cheese. The only cheese that they were permitted to make was Cheddar, although rules were put in place which stated that this variety must not be dyed red with annatto. The Stilton cheese dairies at the time were: Bevamede Dairies at Hickling Pastures (Notts), Nether Broughton, Wymondham; Emberlin & Co. Ltd, Wymeswold; Robert Hames, Church Street, Wymeswold; The Harby Farmers Dairy Ltd, Harby; Henry Knight, Seagrave; Leicester Creameries Ltd, 167 Western Road,

Leicester; Long Clawson Dairy Ltd, Long Clawson; Melton Dairy Farmers, North Street, Melton Mowbray; The Scalford Dairy, Scalford; Stathern and District dairy, Stathern; Tuxford & Tebbutt Ltd, 50 Thorpe End, Melton Mowbray; William Taylor, Wymeswold; United Dairies, Harby; John Watson, Waltham-on-the-Wolds and Webster Dairies, Saxelbye. However, a number of these dairies were not equipped to produce pressed cheese and closed down for the duration of the war. In 1948 some of the closed dairies attempted to reopen, and for the next 30 years there were a series of take overs and closures, although a number of dairies managed to survive to the present day.

Today Stilton cheese can be produced only in the counties of Leicestershire, Nottinghamshire and Derbyshire. Some of the modern producers of Stilton include: Hartington Creamery, Hartington, Buxton; Long Clawson Dairy, Long Clawson, Melton Mowbray, Leicestershire; Tuxford and Tebbutt, Thorpe End, Melton Mowbray; Colston Bassett Dairy, Harby Lane, Colston Bassett, Nottinghamshire; Cropwell Bishop Creamery, Nottingham Road, Cropwell Bishop, Nottinghamshire; Quenby Hall, near Hungarton, Leicestershire and Websters Dairy, Saxelbye, Melton Mowbray, Leicestershire.

In June 1936 the Stilton Cheese Makers' Association was founded to represent the interests of its members. The association also manages the certification trade mark, which protects the name Stilton and authorizes its use only on cheese of the required quality made in the three counties. Stilton cheese has been classified as a 'European Union protected designation of origin product'. In February 1989 the Minister of Agriculture announced at Westminster that he intended to ban the sale of factory-produced unpasteurised cheese, to meet the needs of many importers of cheese from the United Kingdom and because unpasteurised milk could cause illness due to bacteria. Now the Stilton Cheese Makers' Association insists that only pasteurised milk can be used in the production of 21st-century Stilton cheese.

Many historians state that Stilton cheese is a 'new cheese', but this statement could not be further from the truth. The name 'Stilton cheese' for a specific variety became widespread in around 1720. Although a cheese like Stilton had been produced in England as far back as the 12th century, these early versions would have carried the name of the person, village or dairy where they were made. Examples of these cheeses include Whitworth (1618), Lady Beaumont (1630), Berrif (1686) and Scarborough (1700). Cheese produced locally was called 'Cheese from Stilton'. Cream cheese with blue veins imported to this small market town was called Stilton cheese, and again these cheeses varied in quality because of the expanded market. Standardisation was required, and this was achieved by Frances Pawlett and Cooper Thornhill.

It was not until the Stilton Cheese Makers' Association was formed that a true quality cheese materialised. Before World War Two some farmers' cheese sold as Stilton would not meet the health standards required today. The author once spoke to a farmer in his 80s who produced Stilton cheese in the 1930s in the Vale of Belvoir. He had produced cheese in an outbuilding, which he considered to be his dairy. The fresh milk was coagulated in a galvanised bath, and above this container he had suspended the worn-out saddle from one of his horses. Green mould developed on the leather coating, and when he hit the saddle the mould fell into the bath to speed up the growth of blue mould in the cheese!

Presentation of food is everything, and is today as important as it has ever been. In the villages around Melton Mowbray Stilton cheese was, and still is, served after the sweet course at family gatherings. The ritual is that the host introduces the port to their left and Stilton cheese to their right, traditionally served with a silver scoop. Today it is considered wiser to use a Stilton server, which allows the cheese to be cut level in neat wedges, avoiding waste and enabling the cheese to be stored correctly between servings. Port was sometimes introduced into the scooped out base of an aged Stilton cheese. The author actually witnessed this act. The cheese had been scooped out inside the drum, with a few inches of cheese left inside the thick crust. I noticed that mites had been attracted to the cheese and could be seen moving about on the surface. The head of the house then entered and, before passing the wine, poured port into the base of the cheese. The cheese turned pink, and, upon noticing the mites on the cheese, the host commented 'This will steady up these little beggars'!

Today's method of producing Stilton cheese is actually very reminiscent of the process used in the past, although the final product is, in fact, very subtly different. Fine quality milk is delivered to the respective dairy on a daily basis. It is then pasteurised, poured into vats and has starter milk and rennet added. Coagulation then takes place. The curd is cut with a specialised cutter and this releases the whey, which then proceeds to drain from the consolidated curd. The curd is then cut into small blocks and further draining takes place. After it has fully drained the curd is broken up into walnut-shaped portions, to which salt is added, and the crumbled curd is placed into moulds, which are turned twice daily for two days. The white consolidated cheese is then removed from the mould and 'rubbed up' with a flat knife to form a crust. The cheese is then stacked in a maturing room and turned daily. Controlled pressing of the cheese takes place to enable the blue mould to mature evenly throughout the cheese, so creating a marbled effect when the cheese is cut in half. Through pasteurisation bacterial growth in the cheese is safely controlled, and there are a number of contributing factors that produce the blue mould, not least of all the presence of *Penicillium roqueforti* or *Penicillium glaucum*.

Historically, Stilton and Leicestershire cheese are linked through their development in the East Midlands. Through the involvement of bureaucratic cheese advisers the modern Stilton cheese does not match the cheese of the early 1940s. In the author's opinion, Stilton cheese should be produced from unpasteurised milk. Similarly, Leicestershire pressed cheese should be produced from unpasteurised milk. A controlled herd of cows is essential, and they would facilitate the production of a true farmhouse cheese as milk would be tested on site, rather than it being imported from a variety of farms from assorted cows and then pasteurised to produce cheese on factory lines.

A drawing of a carrier's cart conveying cheese to market from a farmhouse dairy in the 19th century. The bull is viewing 'his' cheese leaving the farm.

Students producing Stilton cheese at the Midland Agricultural College Dairy Department at Kingston College, Sutton Bonington, Nottinghamshire, in 1915. The opening of this specialist dairy took place on Tuesday 17 September 1895 by the Duke of Devonshire. His family had supported the production of Midland cheese for many hundreds of years.

From the early 1920s until 1939 considerable expansion took place at the college. In 1935 there were 112 students attending a variety of courses; 55 per cent were sons and daughters of farmers and 74 per cent of all the students came from the contributing counties, which then included the Kesteven Division of Lincolnshire.

World War Two had a devastating effect on the college, with all courses being cancelled in September 1939. Special six-week courses were offered as part of the basic training for Land Army girls, and in January 1940 Ministry of Agriculture-controlled courses were started. The manufacture of Stilton cheese was not included.

In 1946 the National Agricultural Advisory Service was formed, which totally altered the way in which the Sutton Bonington campus was run. In April 1946 the property was transferred from Sutton Bonington to University College Nottingham, and courses involving the actual production of cheese were phased out.

In the photograph two students are working with curd ladles, while two others check the curd strainer bags lying in the 'leads'. Boards, 'bits' and hoops are stacked on the hasteners in the background.

Chapter Six

Stichelton

The present village of Stilton is situated on the line of the Roman road called Ermine Street or the Great North Road. In about AD 45 a trading station was constructed approximately 70 miles north of Londinium by the Romans, on a trackway that existed along the edge of the existing fenland. Archaeology has uncovered an extensive Roman occupation site with sound evidence that cheese was produced locally and marketed to the travelling Romanised populace for over 300 years, reaching its peak by AD 350. After the decline of the Roman empire Saxon traders spread through the east of England, and it is possible that they used the Roman site that is now the village of Stilton as a trading post.

In 586 Creoda was created the first King of Mercia, an area which encompassed all of the Midlands and much of eastern England. He could possibly be considered the first king of England. This Saxon king built churches, small villages and towns throughout Mercia. There was conflict between the pagan factions of the occupying Saxons and those who eventually embraced Christianity. Eventually things settled down and a totally self-sufficient rural economy developed, which became the envy of other northern states of Europe. Anglo-Saxon England was ruled by Church and State combined. This led to the formation of the English parishes, each with a priest and a place of worship.

From 757 to 796 Offa was King of Mercia and defeated the rival claimants to his throne until eventually he controlled most of England south of the Humber. He issued the major form of royal coinage. He erected a defensive earthwork, Offa's Dyke, to keep the warlike Welsh out of England. Farming expanded and cheese produced from ewes' milk was in high demand. During the Roman occupation the local community throughout the country had become soft, allowing the Saxons to take over, and now, after hundreds of years of reasonable peace, with a country devoted to a self-sufficient agricultural economy, the British were open to attack by adventurous invaders. The 'Sea Wolves', Vikings and Danes, began raiding the islands of Britain.

It is possible that it all started after a raid by three longships with around 200 Viking pirates on the Wessex coast. These raiders killed Offa's reeve, stole as much booty as they could and left before any opposition could be formed. At the end of Offa's reign, in about 790, the number of attacks and pillages increased because the coasts of the British Isles offered very easy pickings. The Vikings, Norsemen and the Danes, through continuous raids, pillage and the taking of slaves, particularly females, developed a greater awareness of the soft belly of England and how it could be occupied by controlled invasion.

The control of the countryside by the Danelaw began, a slow process which eventually affected most of Saxon England. Brilliant soldiers, wearing chain mail and carrying long two-handled battleaxes, the Danes were feared throughout

The plundering Danes killing the local Saxon leaders in East Anglia, c.795. They then took over the running of the local farms, especially in what became to be known as the village of Stichiltone. This engraving was published by M.A. Jones in 1829.

Europe. The Danes moved wherever they liked from the sea into estuaries and along the navigable rivers. From many thousands of raids, fighting, plundering and eventually occupying the countryside, the Danes proceeded to occupy England as their permanent home. The Saxon farming peasant, called from his home, leaving his plough and oxen, and with a crude shield and a handmade spear, was no challenge to the north European invaders who were trained in war.

The occupation of England by the Danish invaders was an uncertain time. Saxon leaders were repeatedly defeated in war by the well-trained Danish armies, either by conquest or by gradual infiltration by aggressive occupiers seeking to expand the Danish empire. Resentment of the Danes would have been widespread throughout England, but the Saxon peasant could do little. Opposition to the Danelaw by the Saxons was considerable and resistance was continuous.

King Alfred attempted to control the occupying Danes, but he was never fully successful and died in 918. For the next 40 years England was in turmoil. Battles between Saxons and Danes were regular. Edgar became King in 957 and he attempted to unify the country by making peace with most of the occupying Danes. These Scandinavian warriors brought their children to their new home and became integrated with the Saxons. Danes were a dominant race, and through marriage they became part of the Saxon community. The Danes were fine farmers, and their home country produced fine cheese from cows' milk. They imported fine breeding stock that were hardier than the native cows and could withstand the savage winters of eastern England. Unfortunately, because of the vast fenland to the east, cows were not profitable locally and so sheep farming still took precedence.

In 978 Ethelred II (the Unready) tried to control the country. He was a Saxon with a Danish wife. However, war with the Danish king, Canute, persisted, and eventually Canute fought Ethelred and defeated him. Canute became the Danish King of England from 1014, and for the next 52 years England was ruled by Saxon and Danish families. Despite the fact that the country was in continuous turmoil, farming methods continued to develop. The English wool trade thrived, with woollen goods exported in vast quantities to support the weavers in northern Europe and beyond. In the summer months ewes' milk produced large quantities of cream cheese, which, when stored, developed blue veins.

After Canute's death in 1035 control of England was left to his second son Harold I, who reigned for five years. Hardicanute, King of Denmark, was elected King of England by the Danes and he reigned for two years. When he died Edward the Confessor was elected as king (he was half Saxon, half Danish) and he ruled until 1066. During his lifetime he embraced Roman Catholicism and invited Norman clergy into England. In 1052 Danish landowners rebelled against the elected king, but Norman support helped defeat the uprising. In return for their assistance Edward had stated that on his death a Norman should rule England. However, there was considerable opposition from both Saxons and Danes, neither of which wanted a Norman to rule England. When Edward died Harold II was elected King of England in 1066. William, Duke of Normandy, stated that Edward had promised the crown of England to a Norman. Thus the stage was set for the Norman Conquest. The Danes believed that if anybody should rule England it should be them. Harold II, desperate to hang on to his crown, fought a battle against the Danes at Stamford Bridge, then marched south to fight the Norman occupiers at Senlac near Hastings. Harold and his two sons were killed, and so ended 600 years of Anglo-Saxon and Danish rule of England. A Norman age began when William I became king.

After William the Conqueror's victory over Harold II in 1066 he started to change the method of rule that had developed under Anglo-Saxon law and Danish hostility. His generals were granted large parts of England and if the ruling Saxons or Danes resisted they were killed. If they accepted the new systems and the Norman Conqueror's laws they were integrated into the new system of controls. William had been envious of the wealth of developed farming communities throughout England, which had prospered in spite of centuries of uprisings, civil war and invasions. The people living in the villages, hamlets and isolated communities continued to plant crops and raise produce, especially cattle and, above all, sheep. The income from wool and sheep products, butter and cheese was exceptional. One of the main attractions for the conquest of England was financial gain. Religion and politics were of secondary importance. Strong rule of the occupied country was maintained by William's generals, who introduced his form of taxation, which was designed to support his occupying army and develop Roman Catholicism throughout the country. William instigated a survey of the whole of the country, now known as the *Domesday Book* (1085–86), in which every village, town and city was surveyed. The 'town' of Stilton was no exception. Situated on the important highway 70 miles north of London at the time of the Conquest, it was a very important junction town.

In the *Domesday Book* this 'town' is part of the 'Normancross Hund' in the county of 'Huntedunscire' and is divided into three areas. It is very difficult to determine how much land was awarded to a variety of Norman landowners. The area was under Danish control for many hundreds of years and their system of land measurement differed to that used by the Saxon landowners. Eventually Norman measurements were adopted. In William's survey the local scribes and surveyors used local measures and their own methods to make their assessment. The local Danes objected to Norman rule and this may explain why only one local landowner of Danish/Saxon origin is listed. Called Tovi, he employed six farm workers, had a small herd of cows, approximately one acre of land for raising crops, 16 acres of meadow for raising cows and five acres of woodland. He hired out his farm workers and oxen to plough other farmers' land. Tovi is listed as living in Sticitone, marketing his milk and producing Sticitone cheese for sale in the Normancross Hundred. It is possible that Tovi had been converted to Christianity and supported the Bishop of Lincoln, to whom the king had granted nine farms with their owners to pay taxes to him in this part of the hundred.

William I, when he conquered England, appointed his successful generals to control the whole of the country. He in turn granted land to the Church. He retained land to generate income for his own use, especially if the farm in question showed a good financial return. In Stichitone (Stilton) he farmed over 60 acres, principally to raise sheep, for wool, hides and above all fine cheese made from ewes' milk, a cream cheese with blue veins similar to the cheese of France, Roquefort, a famous cheese in the 11th century that was known throughout Europe.

Eustace the Sheriff, one of William's Norman landowners, had been granted 31 farms, nine of which were in the Normancross Hundred. He paid taxes directly to the King. Eustace appointed a man called John, who came over from France, to run one of his farms. He controlled a large farm of one virgate in size. Under Danish measurement this would have been about 20 acres, and this land was ploughed to raise crops such as wheat and other types of corn. He also had 16 acres of meadow for raising sheep and cows, five acres of wood and six oxen, which could be hired out for ploughing. It would seem that there were at least four rented houses on this land. Two occupiers were allowed to obtain independent work, but two were little better than slaves. It is possible that the two 'freemen' produced and sold cheese. This large farm is recorded as being situated in 'Sticiltone'.

William I retained 10 farms in Huntingdonshire, three of which were in the Normancross Hundred. In the village of Stichiltone he maintained a large farm. He appointed an owner-manager who controlled 30 villages and paid taxes directly to the king. Part of the farm at Stichiltone consisted of a large area of grazing land, which was high ground where sheep were controlled in hurdles. The milk from the sheep was used to produce a cheese not dissimilar to Roquefort. Interestingly, a form of tax (lastage) was obtained from the large expanse of water to the east of Stichitone in the form of eels, which were caught and 'paid' directly to the local abbeys at Lincoln and Ely as 'live' taxes. Traditionally they were eaten by the monks on Fridays.

The Romans made cheese in Stilton and the Saxons and Danes also produced cheese in this town, the making of which was then influenced by the Normans. Evidence shows that a blue-veined cream cheese was made in 'Stichelton', a slightly different spelling to *Domesday Book* references, when the town was under the control of the Bishop of Lincoln in the 14th century.

Some members of the Stilton Cheese Makers' Association infer that Stichelton/Stilton cheese was not in fact made in Stilton. Until the end of the 18th century cheese was made in the many farms surrounding the small town of Stilton. Because the farmland around the village began to be used to raise horses for the coaching trade rather than for livestock, more cheese needed to be made in order to keep the local farms solvent. A standardisation then took place in Leicestershire and the surrounding counties to produce a blue-veined cheese, because of the increased demand. The small farms in Huntingdonshire could not meet the demand because they had not been enclosed to support large herds of cows and most of the grassland was unsuitable. Cows were not as hardy as sheep and they had to be protected throughout the winter months. Sheep lived well on rough grassland, their woollen coats brought in a financial return and their lambs were raised for meat. A milking cow was a large animal and had to produce a calf every year to maintain a continuous supply of milk, so if a cow became barren it was killed. Male calves were killed at birth or shortly after and the meat sold as veal. During the mediaeval period male calves were castrated, and these oxen grew into large powerful animals that were used to pull the ploughs to till farmland.

The finest cheese has always been produced in controlled quantities on the richest grassland. In the 21st century there is an increased demand for good clean organic food that is produced without the use of any additives. Unfortunately, most of the large dairies that produce Stilton cheese manufacture a factory designed cheese. They all use pasteurised milk and they then introduce controlled additives. Until 1989 some dairies were still producing Stilton cheese from unpasteurised milk until the Stilton Cheese Makers' Association insisted that all Stilton cheese must be produced from pasteurised milk. The worry was that because the dairies were making cheese with milk obtained from many different farms it was impossible to control unwelcome bacteria in the purchased milk. The large controlling dairies had no choice but to pasteurise their milk, which is done by heating the milk to neutralise it before controlled bacteria is added along with suitable rennet.

Stilton cheese gained its reputation because it was sold in London in the 1740s, and without the London cheese trade centred on Cornhill this cheese would not have gained its reputation as the finest English cheese. After Cooper Thornhill's death the cheese marketed to London from the small town of Stilton was handled by many organisations. The two major centres for marketing Stilton cheese were the London markets and the great cheese markets held in Leicester. In 1883 the town estate in Melton Mowbray proceeded to organise a Stilton cheese fair, which attracted buyers from all the major cities. These fairs were then held three times a year until the last one was held in 1915. During and after World War One was a very difficult period for the production and sale of Stilton cheese because the process had become commercialised and single farmhouse dairies could not compete. Through the involvement of the director of Long Clawson Dairy situated in the Vale of Belvoir, the Stilton Cheese Makers' Association was formed with its offices in Melton Mowbray. The last farmhouse dairy marketing Stilton cheese was run by Frank Fryer in Somerby near Melton Mowbray in 1935, and he sold his milk directly to a cheese-making dairy. Mrs Doris Wright of Ingorsby Lodge, near Leicester, continued to produce Stilton cheese that had been manufactured in the farmhouse dairy since the 1880s. The Milk Marketing Board controlled the marketing and sale of Stilton cheese after the end of World War Two, but Doris would not agree to national government bureaucracy or the terms offered by the Stilton Cheese Makers' Association. She continued to make her own farmhouse Stilton cheese until 1961. She gave her cheese to her friends and used it as a form of barter with neighbouring farmers.

After World War Two the cheese trade in London changed. The price of cheese was all important, relative to the quality of the product. Very few people can remember the creamy, strong-tasting Stilton cheese produced in and around Melton Mowbray before 1940. Arguably mass production has ruined the quality of all cheeses, not least of all some Stilton cheese, because there is a sense that the character has gone and a bland, ordinary cheese is being produced instead.

In February 1989 the Minister of Agriculture announced that he was going to ban the sale of unpasteurised cheese. On that same day the Specialist Cheesemakers' Association was formed. Randolph Hodson was elected as the first chairman. Unpasteurised cheese was offered for sale at the Sunday Market held at the Spitalfields Market, London, and Randolph Hodson decided to extend this further from a small shop at Covent Garden, eventually opening up Neal's Yard Dairy at Borough Market near London Bridge, south of the River Thames.

Neal's Yard is still the centre in London for a wide variety of excellent cheeses. Cheese is purchased and allowed to mature in the large hastening lofts, to be offered for sale when it reaches maturity. Randolph marketed an excellent Stilton cheese which was produced at Colston Bassett dairy. Unfortunately, against the wishes of the farmers who owned this dairy, the Milk Marketing Board insisted that they must produce all their cheeses from pasteurised milk. Undoubtedly, a Stilton cheese produced from pasteurised milk differs from the farmhouse cheeses that were produced in the 1970s and certainly before World War Two. Many people feel that it differs for the worse. Along with the many other organic cheeses that he marketed, Randolph wished to factor an unpasteurised Stilton cheese through a very fine cheese-maker, Joe Schreider,

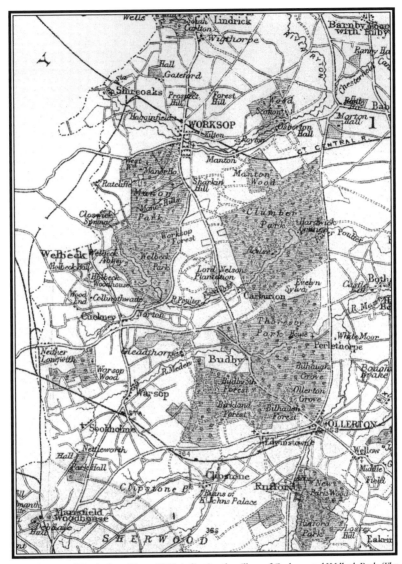

Part of a map of Nottinghamshire, c.1895, indicating the village of Cuckney and Welbeck Park. The Welbeck estate gained international recognition due to the devotion of the 5th Duke of Portland (1854–79) in running an extensive farming estate. He supported modern farming methods at the height of Victorian splendour. His home was Welbeck Abbey and he employed many thousands of men, who, with their families, lived very well. The farms were equipped with the most modern horticultural and farming machinery and were run to the highest standard possible. He owned herds of cows producing high-quality milk, which was processed in an extensive purpose-built dairy. This dairy may have produced and sold soft cheese, curd cream and colwick's, an easily produced cheese made from 'old' coagulated milk, which can be eaten on the same day as its manufacture.

Part of the herd of 150 Friesian-Holstein cows controlled and managed by Mick Lingard, a fine herdsman, in September 2008.

who had produced excellent cheese in the West Country in England and for a number of years in Holland. Together they considered that they should endeavour to produce a traditional Stilton cheese, as close as possible to the historic cheese that was classed as the 'King of English Cheese' before it was commercialised in large factories. They decided to call this traditional style of cheese Stilchelton cheese.

Pasteurisation through heating the milk destroys the harmless bacteria that are present. Stilton cheese is produced by adding a bacterial culture produced in a laboratory. When discussing the manufacture of farmhouse cheese with many producers throughout England, Randolph and Joe decided to produce a Stilton cheese from organic milk. They considered pasteurisation unnecessary because the cheese would be made from milk obtained on a single farm, where the cows and milk would be continuously tested.

Fine herds of cows raised on organically controlled grassland were essential, and after much research Joe Schneider, with the help of Randolph, obtained a tenancy on Collingthwaite Farm on the Welbeck estate in Nottinghamshire, which was in the county covered by the European Union as a protected area. The farms on this estate raise crops and meadows organically and therefore artificial chemicals are not added to the farmed areas. Interestingly, the surplus whey at this farm was mixed with natural effluent obtained from the crew yards where the cows were milked, and this drained into a controlled reservoir where it was mixed and used as a dressing on the meadows.

The Stichelton cheese produced at Collingthwaite Farm is based on recipes used to produce Stilton cheese that date from before 1989 and using similar equipment obtained from the industry. The dairy meets all the requirements of

Nottinghamshire health authority. The cheese produced uses traditional cultures: milk is poured into the vat, with the correct starter, and the cheese develops micro-organisms which eventually form a blue filament throughout the cheese. The normal blue cheese is manufactured on similar lines to Stilton cheese production. Because the cheese is made from unpasteurised milk, a different crust is formed. In the opinion of the author, after about 12 weeks this Stichelton cheese tastes very similar to the cheese marketed in the village of Wymondham (the centre for Stilton cheese production) in 1939. The crust is much thinner, possibly because it is not wrapped in a calico binder and then stored for six months in a loft.

Why then can this blue cheese not be called Stilton? Stichiltone should perhaps be the correct name for a cheese linked with the present village of Stilton. After all, it is following the traditional methods of cheese-making, which were introduced many years before the manufacture of the more mainstream Stilton cheese. It is possible that the first Stichiltone cheese was made in small wooden hoops, whereas the famous Stilton cheese-maker living in Wymondham in the 18th century, Frances Pawlett, used ceramic hoops, very similar to the Roquefort moulds used in southern France.

A Friesian-Holstein. 'I am ready for milking'.

History always repeats itself, and this also applies to cheese production. Stichelton or Stilton cheese could taste similar to cheese that was allowed to mature and was marketed during the Roman occupation, the Anglo-Saxon period and the Norman Conquest, and it may even taste similar to the cheese made up to the middle of the 20th century. It is the commercial demands which have changed the manufacture of the 'cheese of Stilton'. Joe and Randolph are attempting to produce an historic cheese that can be dated back for over 1,000 years, complies with modern standards of production and meets all the 21st-century health, hygiene and safety requirements. This Stichelton cheese captures the flavour of the pastures of fine organic grass grown on the Welbeck Estate and is quite different from the variety of cheese known as Stilton, despite the apparent similarities. The address of this historic dairy is Stichelton Dairy, Collingthwaite Farm, Cuckney, Mansfield, Nottinghamshire.

The author and Joe Schneider at the entrance to Stichelton Dairy at Collingthwaite Farm, Cuckney, in September 2008.

The exterior of the Stichelton Dairy at Collingthwaite Farm, Cuckney.

Joe Schneider cutting the curd, September 2008. Undertaken one and a half hours after the rennet has been added, this process releases the whey which is then drained off.

The curd has been passed through a milling machine and is then carefully placed in plastic hoops. In this photograph the curd has settled and surplus whey has drained through the holes in the mould/hoop.

Joby Williams rubbing up a Stichelton cheese.

Stichelton cheese maturing in the 'loft' in the dairy at Collingthwaite Farm.

A mature Stichelton cheese.

Cheese on a sampling iron that has been used to extract a sample from a Stichelton cheese.

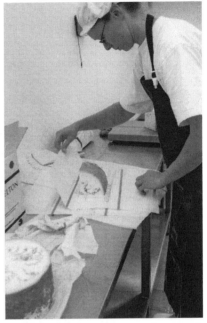

Tracey Scotthorne with a mature Stichelton cheese at the dairy of Collingthwaite Farm in October 2008.

Tracey Scotthorne wrapping a recently cut sample of Stichelton Cheese.

Michael Boyle in the Welbeck Farm Shop, which retails Stichelton cheese.

Welbeck Abbey, c.1930. This building was originally constructed as a Premonstratensian house in 1153–54 and was considered to be the centre of this order by 1512. After the dissolution of the estate and house by Henry VIII very little of the original building remained. The undercroft is one of the pieces that survived and is dated to c.1250. There is an old doorway that can be dated to about 1188. By 1597 Gilbert Talbot had purchased the house from Sir Charles Cavendish, and for the next 150 years considerable demolition and building alterations took place.

In 1744 the then owner, Lady Oxford, commissioned the garden designer Francis Richardson to lay out new gardens and construct the existing lake. Repton was employed in 1790 to lay out more gardens and extend and deepen the lake.

The present house is essentially Victorian, principally because of the remodelling efforts of the 5th Duke of Portland. He commissioned various local builders to demolish and rebuild much of the house, outbuildings and driveways from 1860 onwards. The 6th duke took over the house in 1879 and some changes were made to the gardens. He commissioned Lady Bolsover to finish most of the work taken on by the 5th duke. The house passed through a stable period until a disastrous fire in 1900, which caused much damage to the interior of the house and the exterior façade. For many years work took place on the building. In 1930 the Marquis of Tichfield completed much of the outstanding restoration.

The dairy constructed on the instructions of the 5th Duke of Portland, on the site of a previous dairy.

In the 12th century an abbey was constructed on the Welbeck estate. A dairy would have been built to produce cheese for local consumption. All religious houses supported the local community after the Norman Conquest. It is not beyond the bounds of possibility that a cream cheese was produced and distributed to a much wider area. When Henry VIII dissolved this abbey cheese production continued, as it had at the manor house at Kirby Bellars near Melton Mowbray. In Richard Bradley's book of 1726 covering Stilton cheese production, John Warner has advised him that a type of Stilton cheese was made in Nottinghamshire during the 1600s. Was this an unpressed cream cheese that developed blue veins? Unfortunately, a cartulary covering this abbey has not been located. If a Norman recipe similar to Roquefort was produced in this area between the years 1153–54, eventually to be sold at the town of Stilton, then this would be the first use of the name of Stilton as a Midlands-produced, unpressed, blue-veined cream cheese.

The town of Stilton was an important trading post 70 miles north of London, to which goods from Boston were delivered – a distance that was no longer than from the dairy at Welbeck, which had a direct route to Stilton down Ermine Street. Randolph Hodson and Joe Schneider could be producing a cream cheese where the original unpressed cream cheese was produced. When it developed blue veins and arrived at Stilton it was named Stilton cheese.

The 5th Duke of Portland spent millions of pounds constructing examples of the latest Victorian technology. From his home he lined the estate with over two and half miles of underground drives, which cover most of the park. The largest of these tunnels were wide enough for two horse-drawn carriages to pass side by side. All of these tunnels were lit by plate glass skylights and gas lamps. The Duke even constructed his own purpose-built gas works using his own coal. In this photograph a horse and trap is leaving one of the tunnels in 1904, after delivering milk to buildings on the estate.

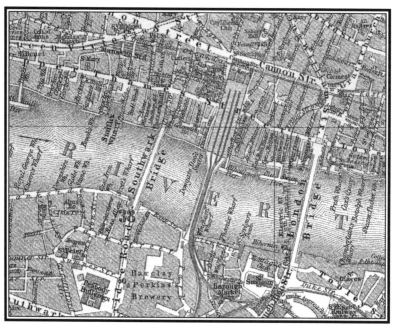

Borough Market, south of the River Thames, near the church of St Saviours and London Bridge, c.1905. The market was one of the largest wholesalers in London, marketing farm products, fruit and vegetables. It led into the London 'Corn Exchange'.

The 'Exchange' leading into Lombard Street, London, 1904.

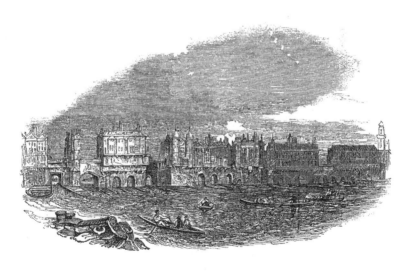

London Bridge as it looked in 1760, connecting the famous markets with the city of London.

Borough Market in October 2008.

Neal's Yard Dairy at Borough Market in October 2008.

Trevor Hickman and Randolph Hodgson discussing cheese production in Neal's Yard Dairy, surrounded by a wide variety of English cheeses, October 2008.

Trevor Hickman with a round of Sparkenhoe Red Leicester cheese and Randolph Hodgson holding half of a Stichelton cheese.

A fine display of Stichelton cheese on offer in Neal's Yard Dairy. This cheese is made from unpasteurised organic cows' milk using a traditional animal rennet.

Jo Shimkus cutting Sparkenhoe Red Leicester cheese on sale in Neal's Yard Dairy in October 2008. This is just one of the many cheeses sold in this dairy that are produced from unpasteurised milk.

Postscript

After compiling my book *The History of Stilton Cheese* I proceeded to write a further book involving food, *The History of the Melton Mowbray Pork Pie*. Both of these books have been reprinted. While undertaking my research for these two publications I was given considerable help by many people. I have duly made acknowledgements in these two publications. When I was researching my book about the Melton Mowbray Pork Pie in 1996, Mitch Farquharson of Tuxford & Tebbutt provided me with a large amount of information about the production of pies in Melton Mowbray and further information on Stilton cheese. Tuxford & Tebbutt were producing Red Leicester cheese in their dairy, and he suggested that I should write a book about this county's famous cheese.

My research on the history of Leicestershire, Derbyshire and Nottinghamshire cheese has taken many years. For example, with the help of my granddaughter, Amy Grech, I visited all of the villages and hamlets in the Sparkenhoe Hundred, where a local cheese had been made for centuries. Through my research I uncovered a lot more information on Stilton cheese and, of course, I was able to compile a short history of Leicestershire cheese. I have finally collated my research and have presented an account of these cheeses in this book. I feel that it is appropriate that I name the historic characters from the past, without whose foresight I could not have compiled this publication: the pioneers of the Stilton cheese industry, Frances Pawlett, Cooper Thornhill, Thomas Nuttall and Henry Morris. Another person who ranks highly in the history of cheese production in Leicestershire is Shuckburgh Ashby, a farming entrepreneur dealing in pressed cheese near Hinckley. When Leicestershire cheese production was at its peak he decided to move away in order to produce and market Stilton cheese from Quenby Hall in 1759. Much of the historic past of the area was uncovered when I browsed through the extensive survey of the district centred on the town of Hinckley by John Nichols, which was published in two volumes – in 1783 *The*

LM01

FRIDAY, JANUARY 30, 2009

NEWS

DISCOVERY: HISTORIAN SAYS ANCIENT RECIPE

King of cheeses from here? No

An ancient recipe for Stilton cheese discovered online has led one historian to challenge Leicestershire's long-held claim as the home of the world-famous cheese.

by **OLIVER WRIGHT**

Richard Landy came across the recipe dating back to 1721 as part of his research into the Bell Inn, in Stilton, Cambridgeshire.

However, experts have dismissed it, saying that the recipe was for a pressed cheese, whereas Stilton is not made in a press.

The recipe was found in a book published in 1726 called A General Treatise of Husbandry and Gardening.

A letter contained in the book from horticulturalist John Warner to Richard Bradbury, professor of botany at Cambridge University, is entitled "Recipe to Make Stilton Cheese".

Mr Landy, 50, from Stilton, believes this is proof that the cheese originated in Cambridgeshire and he was seeking to have the village included in the list of creameries authorised by law to make the cheese.

At present, the widely accepted story behind the cheese is that it was first made in the 18th century, specifically around the Melton Mowbray area and taken to be sold at The Bell Inn, in Stilton, by Frances Pawlett, from Wymondham. It was called Stilton because it was served there.

Mr Landy said: "The roads at the time were atrocious, so why would Leicestershire farmers drag tonnes of cheese 40 or 50 miles just to sell it and make somebody else famous?

"Frances Pawlett came into the equation much later when the pub could not cope with the demand."

He said that his calls for Stilton to be recognised officially as the home of the cheese have been

1721 RECIPE FOR STILTON CHEESE

The recipe, complete with original grammar, spelling and punctuation:

Take ten gallons of Morning Milk, and five gallons of sweet Cream, and beat them together; then put in as much boiling Spring-water, as will make it warmer than Milk from the Cow; when this is done, put in Runnet made strong with large Mace, and when it is come (or the Milk is set in Curd) break it as small as you would do for Cheese-Cakes; and after that salt it, and put it into the Fatt, and press it for two hours. Then boil the Whey, and when you have taken off the Curds, put the Cheese into the Whey, and let it stand half an Hour; then put it in the Press, and when you take it out, bind it up for the first Fortnight in Linen Rollers, and turn it upon Boards for the first Month twice a Day.

CASTS DOUBT ON REAL HOME OF STILTON

is not whey!

backed by Lord Mawhinney, former Tory MP and chairman of the Football League.

Since Mr Landy's discovery Stilton expert Trevor Hickman rejected the significance of the recipe. He said this week: "This is a recipe that the landlord of the Bell Inn at Stilton held and it was how you made a cheese in Stilton. But this was for a pressed cheese, whereas Stilton is not a pressed cheese."

Mr Landy hit back saying he has found several recipes from the 18th and 19th century which all mention a press or pressing.

In relation to his own discovery, he said: "What you have to remember is that the man who wrote down this recipe was a horticulturalist, not a cheesemaker and his use of language may be somewhat different."

RESEARCH: A recipe for Stilton from 1721 casts doubt on the real home of the cheese, according to historian Richard Landy

Supplied Courtesy of The Leicester Mercury.

History and Antiquities of Hinckley and in 1790 *The History and Antiquities of the Town and County of Leicester.* James Thompson's book *The History of Leicester* published in 1849 also proved to be very useful.

When compiling books such as this you expect criticism and advice. What I find annoying, however, is modern reporters who publish inaccurate comments without any sound research. One frequent example is that they seem unable to differentiate between the factoring and manufacturing of cheese. Another common misconception is that Cooper Thornhill married the cook at Quenby Hall or Frances Pawlett's daughter. He did neither. Nor did he live in Leicestershire. Stilton cheese was not invented at Quenby Hall but in the town of Stilton in Huntingdonshire and later developed in Leicestershire. In a recent *Factfile* published in a local newspaper it stated that two types of pressed cheese, Leicester and Leicestershire, were not produced. According to the article all cheese was called 'Leicestershire Cheese' and was renamed Red Leicester after 1945. This is another example of a reporter stretching the truth.

In 1994 I met Alan Salt, a fine Stilton cheese-maker at Hartington dairy in Derbyshire. We became very good friends, and with him I try to keep the record straight regarding the history of cheese production in Leicestershire. Alan travels throughout Great Britain, Europe and the US promoting English cheese. With both his knowledge and the historical evidence that I have uncovered included within these pages I consider this to be a reasonable record of the production of three types of historic cheese in the centre of England. I hope you have enjoyed reading it.

Trevor Hickman